AF454249

The Holy Spirit's Presence

Accessing God's Power by Acknowledging Our Weakness

A. W. Tozer
& Caleb Sinclair

GRAPEVINE INDIA

Published by

GRAPEVINE INDIA PUBLISHERS PVT LTD

www.grapevineindia.com
Delhi | Mumbai
email: grapevineindiapublishers@gmail.com

Ordering Information:
Quantity sales: Special discounts are available on quantity
purchases by corporations, associations, and others.
For details, reach out to the publisher.

First published by Grapevine India 2022

Introduction

It is a truth firmly established in the Bible that the sin-caused gulf between man and God cannot be closed by any effort on our part. God Himself must make the move of restoration. This He has done first through the incarnation of His Son, and then by the indwelling of the Holy Spirit. The Spirit's role in redemption cannot be duplicated by any human effort.

There are vast and varied views on the Holy Spirit today. Only the preacher who speaks from the Bible, quoting chapter and verse, is valid and true. In Tozer, we find a man who is Spirit-filled and burning with a spiritual desire to spread God's truth. He touches upon the divine nature of the Holy Spirit and His importance in the life of the spiritual man.

We can never know all about the mysterious workings of the Spirit, he admits. Instead, he seeks to reassure the reader of what can be known, and to incite us to worship and surrender. Through this book, may you, dear reader, learn the life of trust—trust in the Holy Spirit to lead you through life in a way that magnifies God.

– Caleb Sinclair

Divine Help

Man Aspires for Greatness

Everything in the natural world falls short of man's supreme aspiration for God and His presence. You do not have to like it, but we might as well face up to it: We are the glory and the rubbish of the universe; but we never would have been the rubbish of the universe if we had not chosen the gutter. If sin had not entered the world, and we had not fallen, we would never have been the rubbish of the universe. We would have been the glory of the universe.

When our Lord is finished with His redemptive work, He will have made His people, once again, the glory of the universe, when He comes to be admired in His saints and glorified in all them that see Him.

Man is the weakest creature there is, but he is the only creature that knows how weak he is. That is where his glory lies: in his weakness. He is able to know how weak he is, and no other creature knows this.

I do not suppose that if you were to ask a mosquito, "Are you weak?" he would say yes. He does not know he is weak. He could not answer you. He would not know what you said. If mosquitoes could talk, they would call us the animal that swats, because that is the only thing that they know about us.

Man is the unknown—pitiful, wonderful, weak, mysterious—and yet he is the only creature that knows he is this. Man is the only creature that sins, and yet he is the only creature that could know that he sins. And man is the only creature that knows how foolish and inconsistent he is, and he laughs at himself. He is the only creature that aspires, because there is no other creature dissatisfied with himself. Man alone is dissatisfied with himself.

In John Keats's poem "Ode to a Nightingale," he made this point, among other very wonderful things: You were here. You were here way back long ago when the Grecians heard thee sing among the isles of Greece. Yes, the nightingale was there then, but the nightingale was there before there was any Greece, and before there was any

Egypt.

Why has the nightingale remained the nightingale from the time God created her and said, "Let the birds inhabit the air"? Because the nightingale, although she is a beautiful singer, does not aspire. But the man who used to come out of his cave and listen to a nightingale is now dressed in a Hart, Schaffner & Marx suit and watches television. Why? He has aspired, you see. He has come up. Only man aspires. All other creatures are exactly what they were; the only creature that ever improves is the one that man gets hold of and crossbreeds.

Those Guernsey, Jersey, Holstein and Hereford cattle you see standing around in little clusters under the trees on hot days are crossbreeds. They have been bred up to that. Someone got a hold of a poor swayback heifer and bred her to something better. Then he bred that to something better, and on until he has these fine cattle. If man can get hold of a thing, he will breed it up, because man alone aspires. Nothing else aspires. The lowly cow does not aspire to be anything more or else than she is.

What does this indicate? It indicates that God made man in His own image, and in the image and likeness of God made He him, and of nothing else can this be said.

Therefore, man aspires and is the only creature that prays and worships. God made man to worship, and he is the only creature that God made to worship, at least the only creature down here. The lion roars for his prey and the bird builds its nest in the thickets. The stormy wind fulfills God's will, and He gives hail and snow like wool. Snow does not pray, and neither does the bird pray; neither does the lion pray, and neither does the stormy wind pray. We can read prayer into it, but it is not there until we read it in. We, who can pray, read into nature prayers, and we say the wind is moaning her prayers to heaven, but she is only moaning in our imagination. The wind is just blowing. You and I are doing the moaning. So we read those thoughts into nature.

We say the little bird dips his bill in the water, then looks up and thanks God for it, but the bird is merely putting his chin up so the water will run down. That is all, purely a mechanical thing. No bird prays. I think it is perfectly terrible to get a dog down beside the bed and have him pray, as some people do. If God made a dog to pray, he would be praying without your getting him down alongside your bed, so stop it if you have been doing it. No dog ever prayed. No bird ever prayed. It is man alone that prays.

God's Goodness

Thou art good, and doest good.

PSALM 119:68

I will mention the lovingkindnesses of the LORD, and the praises of the LORD, according to all that the LORD hath bestowed on us, and the great goodness toward the house of Israel, which he hath bestowed on them according to his mercies, and according to the multitude of his lovingkindnesses.

ISAIAH 63:7

How precious also are thy thoughts unto me, O God! how great is the sum of them!

PSALM 139:1

For the LORD will again rejoice over thee for good.

DEUTERONOMY 30:9

How excellent is thy lovingkindness, O God! therefore the children of men put their trust under the shadow of thy wings.

PSALM 36:7

O taste and see that the LORD is good.

PSALM 34:8

If ye then, being evil, know how to give good gifts unto your children, how much more shall your Father which is in heaven give good things to them that ask him?

MATTHEW 7:11

I have for over thirty years spoken about God's goodness. It is most important that we know about God's goodness and know what kind of God He is. What is God like? It is a question that must be answered if we're going to be any kind of Christians at all. Don't take that for granted and say, "I already know."

There are those that say religion is something grafted onto man that is the result of man's weakness or superstition. However, history shows that no tribe or nation has ever risen morally above its religion. If it had a debased religion, it had a debased people. If the people were not debased, the religion, though neither Christianity nor Judaism, nevertheless was relatively high in the scale of non-revealed religions.

And remember that no religion has ever risen above its conception of God. If the heathen believe that God is tricky, sulky, nasty and deceitful, their religion will build itself around that concept. And they will try to be sneaky with their god and act the way their god acts.

If they believe, on the other hand, that God is one God, that He is a high and true and noble God, then even though they are not redeemed, their religion will tend to follow their concept of God upward, even though it is a pagan religion and does not carry redemption.

Christianity at any given time is strong or weak depending upon her concept of God. And I insist upon this and I have said it many times, that the basic trouble with the Church today is her unworthy conception of God. I talk with learned and godly people all over the country, and they're all saying the same thing.

Unbelievers say, "Take your cowboy god and go home," and we get angry and say, "They're vile heathen." No, they're not vile heathen— or at least that's not why they say that. They can't respect our "cowboy god." And since evangelicalism has gone overboard to "cowboy religion," its conception of God is unworthy of Him.

Our religion is little because our god is little. Our religion is weak because our god is weak. Our religion is ignoble because the god we serve is ignoble. We do not see God as He is.

The psalmist said, "*O magnify the LORD with me.*" (Psalms 34:3)

"Magnify" may mean one of two things: "make it look bigger than it is," or "see it as big as it is." The latter is what "magnify" means as the psalmist used it.

If you want to examine a very small amount of matter, you put it under a microscope and magnify it to make it look bigger than it is. But it is impossible to make God look bigger than He is. When we say "magnify the Lord," we mean try to see God somewhere near as big as He is. This is what I want to do. This is what, by His help, I have dedicated myself to do.

A local church will only be as great as its conception of God. An individual Christian will be a success or a failure depending upon what he or she thinks of God. It is critically important that we have a knowledge of the Holy One, that we know what God is like. Of course we can know from the Scriptures—that's where we go to get our information. We can know some of it from nature too: "*The heavens declare the glory of God; and the firmament showeth his handiwork.*" (Psalm 19:1) But while the pen of nature writes without too much clarity, the Word of God is very, very clear.

It is very important that we know that God is good. We read that God is good and doeth good and that His lovingkindness is over all His works, and all of those passages of Scripture quoted above. Take a concordance and look up the word "good" or the word "lovingkindness" and see how much the Bible, both the Old and New Testaments, has to say about God being kindhearted.

God is kindhearted, gracious, good-natured and benevolent in intention. And let us remember that God is cordial. We only think we believe, really. We are believers in a sense, and I trust that we believe sufficiently to be saved and justified before His grace. But we don't believe as intensely and as intimately as we should. If we did, we would believe that God is a cordial God, that He is gracious and that His intentions are kind and benevolent. We would believe that God never thinks any bad thoughts about anybody, and He never had any bad thoughts about anybody.

Now all this that I have said means that God is good. All this He is *infinitely*. Why do I say that? Because infinitude is an attribute of God. And it is impossible for God to be anything and not be completely, infinitely what He is. It is possible for the sun to be bright, but not infinitely bright because it doesn't have all the light there is. It is possible for a mountain to be large but not infinitely large. It is possible for an angel to be good, but not infinitely good. Only God can claim infinitude.

When I say that God is good, that God has a kind heart, I mean that

He has a heart infinitely kind and that there is no boundary to it. When I say that God is good-natured, good and kindly of nature, I mean that He is infinitely so.

God is not only infinitely good; He is perfectly good. God is never partway anything! When I say that God is kindhearted, I mean that He is perfectly so. I do not mean that there are ever times when God isn't feeling good and isn't kind.

There are never any times when God won't be cordial. Even the best Christian doesn't always feel cordial. Sometimes he didn't sleep well, and though he's not mad and he's living like a Christian, he doesn't feel like talking in the mornings. He doesn't feel cordial; he's not overflowing; he's not enthusiastic. But there's never a time when God isn't. Because what God is, He is perfectly.

I joyously announce to you that what God is, He is immutably. God never changes. What God was, God is. What God is and was, God will be. There will never be any change in God. Don't call me a heretic; check on me. Go to the Word and see if it's right. If you'll be a good Berean and go to the Scriptures to see if these things are true (see Acts 17:10-11), then that's all I ask.

Remember that God is enthusiastic about His works. God is not an absentee engineer running His world by remote control. The Scripture says that He is "upholding all things by the word of his power" (Hebrews 1:3). The presence of the invisible Word in the universe makes things run. God is the perfect creator and He runs everything by being present in His works. That's all through the prophets, the Psalms and the book of Job—all through the Old Testament.

When we hit the age of science, we forgot that. We have "laws" now. The Bible knew nothing about "the laws of nature." The Bible knew only that God was there. If it rained, it was God watering His hills from His chambers. If there was lightning, it was God, and if there was thunder, it was the "voice of the LORD" that "maketh the hinds to calve" (Psalm 29:9).

The writers of Scripture were acutely God-conscious, and they were never lonely because God was there. "Surely the LORD is in this place; and I knew it not," said Jacob (Genesis 28:16). This idea that God is an absentee engineer running His universe by remote control is all wrong. He is present in perpetual and continuous eagerness, with all the fervor of rapturous love pressing His holy designs. If you don't feel that way about it, it's unbelief that makes you feel other-wise; it's preoccupation with this world. If you would believe God, you would know this to be true.

The goodness of God means He cannot feel indifferent about any-thing. People are indifferent, but not God. God either loves with a boundless unremitting energy or He hates with consuming fire. It was said about the second Person of the Trinity, *"Thou hast loved righteousness, and hated iniquity; therefore God, even thy God, hath anointed thee with the oil of gladness above thy fellows."* (Hebrews 1:9)

The same Lord Jesus that loved with boundless consuming love also hated with terrible consuming fire and will continue to do so while the ages roll. The goodness of God requires that God cannot love sin.

The goodness of God is the only valid reason for existence, the only reason underlying all things. Do you imagine that you deserve to be born, that you deserve to be alive? The unbelieving poet Omar Khayyám said,

> *Into this universe and why*
>
> *not knowing nor whence*
>
> *like water willy-nilly flowing*
>
> *and out of it like wind along the waste,*
>
> *whither I know not,*
>
> *willy-nilly blowing.*

And then He charged God with it all and said, "For all that I've done that's wrong, O God, forgive and take my forgiveness." He thought God owed him something. But remember that you can answer every question with this expression: "God of His goodness willed it. God out of His kindness willed it."

Why were we created? Was it that we deserved to be created? How can nothing deserve something? There was a time when there was no human race. How therefore could a human race that hadn't ex-isted deserve something? How could a man that wasn't yet created earn anything or pile up any merit? It couldn't be so. God out of His goodness created us. Why were we not destroyed when we sinned?

The only answer is that God of His goodness spared us. The cordial, kind-intentioned God spared us.

Why would God the Eternal Son bleed for us? The answer is, out of His goodness and lovingkindness. *"Therefore the children of men put their trust under the shadow of thy wings."* *(*Psalm 36:7*)*

Why would God forgive me when I've sinned and then forgive me again and again? Because God out of His goodness acts according to that goodness and does what His loving heart dictates that He do.

Why does God answer prayer? Let's not imagine that it's because somebody was good. We Protestants think we don't believe in saints, but we do. We canonize them: we have Saint George Mueller, Saint C.H. Spurgeon, Saint D.L. Moody and Saint A. B. Simpson. We get the idea that God answered prayer for them because they were really good. They would deny that fervently if they were here.

Nobody ever got anything from God on the grounds that he deserved it. Having fallen, man deserves only punishment and death. So, if God answers prayer, it's because God is good. From His goodness, His lovingkindness, His good-natured benevolence, God does it! That's the source of everything.

These are the only grounds upon which anybody has ever been saved since the beginning of the world. There is an idea abroad that in the Old Testament men were saved by law and that in the New Testament we are saved by grace. The second is right, but the first is wrong. Nobody has ever been saved, from the day that Abel offered his bloody lamb on a homemade altar, down to the latest convert made today, except out of the goodness of God.

Because of God's grace, His mercy, His lovingkindness, His goodness and graciousness, His cordiality and approachability, He kindly saved people. We've taken the word "grace" and made a technical term out of it.

The people in the Old Testament were not saved by keeping anything, because we deserved hell, and if God had acted according to justice alone, He simply would have pulled the stopper out and flushed us all down to hell and been done with it. But God out of His lovingkindness graciously forgave those who would come according to the conditions God laid down. Everybody is saved by grace.

Abel was saved by grace. Noah was saved by grace— *"Noah found grace in the eyes of the LORD.*" (Genesis 6:8) So was Moses and all the rest down to the coming of Jesus and His dying on the cross. All were saved by grace out of the goodness of God. And everybody's been saved by grace out of the goodness of God ever since.

But let's not drown in all the syrup. God is not only good; God is severe. Romans 11:22 tells us about the severity of God: "*Behold therefore the goodness and severity of God.*" And it says that because Israel turned away from God, God was severe with Israel and temporarily broke her off from the good olive tree and grafted in the Gentiles instead. And so behold the goodness and severity of God.

God is good toward all who accept His goodness. And for those who reject His goodness, there's nothing that even the Almighty God can do if He's going to allow man his free will—and I believe in free will. Free will was given as a gift of God—He's given us a little provisional sovereignty out of His absolute sovereignty. He has said, "I'll allow you, within a little framework, to be your own boss and to choose to go to heaven or to hell." If a man will not take God's goodness, then he must have God's severity toward all who continue in moral revolt against the throne of God and in rebellion against the virtuous laws of God.

There is nothing God can do and so His justice disposes of all such.

But what about those who have surrendered to His love? God, being holy as well as good, righteous as well as kindly, and we being the sinners we are, are we not of necessity lost? Must we not perish? Is it not moral logic that we should perish?

Let me quote from the book by Lady Julian: "God of His goodness has ordained means to help us, full, fair and many; the chief being that which He took upon Him, the nature of man." In coming to earth as a man, God came where we were, and by coming where we were He understands us by sympathy and empathy.

Sympathy is a good old-fashioned country word: *-pathy* has the same root as *pathos*, which means "feeling or suffering often"; *sym* means "together," such as in the word *symphony* (a group of musicians playing *together* in harmony). Sympathy, then, is God feeling and suffering along with us.

Empathy, of course, is a bit different. It means the ability to project yourself into somebody else and feel as he feels. It is a wonderful theme, and every old grandmother on any old farm in Tennessee knows what empathy means. But it took a good scientist to give it a name.

Let me read it for you from the Bible—in biblical language instead of in the language of psychology:

Wherefore in all things it behoved him [that is, when He took on Him the seed of Abraham] to be made like unto his brethren, that he might be a merciful and faithful high priest in things pertaining to God, to make reconciliation for the sins of the people. For in that he himself hath suffered being tempted, he is able to succour them that are tempted. (Hebrews 2:17-18)

We have not an high priest which cannot be touched with the feeling of our infirmities; but was in all points tempted like as we are, yet without sin. Let us therefore come boldly unto the throne of grace, that we may obtain mercy, and find grace to help in time of need. (4:15-16)

These are passages full of empathy. Not only does He feel along with us in our wretchedness, but He is also able to project Himself into us, so He knows how we feel and can feel with us. That is good theology.

Now God of His goodness has ordained means, "full, fair and many." And it was all out of God's goodness. We say sometimes, "The justice of God requires Him to do so and so." Never use that language— even if you hear me using it! There is never anything that *requires* God to do anything. God does what He does because of what He is, and there is not something standing outside of Him requiring Him to do something. He does what He does out of His own heart. All the attributes of God are simply facets of one God in three Persons.

What are these "full, fair and many" means God has made for His people? They are the precious amends that He's made for man's sins, "turning all our blame into endless worship."

Sometimes I say things to God in prayer which are terribly bold, almost arrogant, and I've never been rebuked by God yet. They said about Luther (I'm certainly not drawing any comparison; I'd have been glad to clean his shoes and put them at his bedroom door!) that when they heard him pray it was an experience in theology. When he began to pray, he prayed with such self-abnegation, such humility, such repentance that you pitied him. But as he prayed on, he prayed with such boldness that you feared for him.

Sometimes in my private prayers I've gone to God with thoughts that I hesitate to mention, but I'm going to mention this one. Only last Friday I said to God in prayer: "I'm glad I sinned, God; I'm glad I sinned, for Thou didst come to save sinners" (see 1 Timothy 1:15).

I'm not a good man; I'm a—well, you'd have to use slang to describe me! By nature I come that way. And when I saw it in my boys, I didn't blame them. I paddled them, but I didn't blame them. I can't go to God and say, "God, I didn't do what that fellow did." I've done everything—either in actuality or in thought—that could be done. The devil himself couldn't have thought of anything that I haven't thought of in my lifetime.

So I was praying to God about it and I said, "O God, these good men"—and I began naming men who, compared with me, are good men—"they can't love You as much as I do, for he who is forgiven much loves much" (see Luke 7:47).

If a doctor saves a man who has only a runny nose, he wouldn't write a book about it. He didn't do much. The fellow would get well anyhow. But the doctor who takes a man with a brain tumor, puts him asleep and, with great care, prayer and skill, brings that man back to life—he has done something.

He "saved a wretch like me." He "turned all our blame into endless worship." I believe the Bible teaches—our Lord hinted at it and Paul developed it further—that the day will come when they will gather around us from everywhere, and say, "Behold the marvels of God." You read in the book of Acts (Acts 4:14) of seeing the man that was healed standing among them, and they could say nothing. And seeing that wicked sinner standing there, we can only say, "Worthy is the Lamb that was slain" (Revelation 5:12). And worthy is the goodness of God that out of His infinite kindness, His unchanging, perfect lovingkindness, He made amends for us, "full, fair and many," turning all our sin into endless worship.

Jesus is God. And Jesus is the kindest man ever to live on this earth. His kindness is something we must have. It must be a reflection, a lingering flavor, like an old vase that once held beautiful flowers. Though the vase is broken, the scent of the roses hangs round the vase. So mankind, fallen like a broken vase, dashed to the pavement and splintered into a million pieces, yet has something we call kindness.

I suppose one of the kindest men in America was Lincoln. When Lincoln visited the hospital there lay a young Northern officer so badly wounded that it was obvious that he was going to die. The nurses whispered, "Mr. President, he can't make it." And the great big, tall, homely president went into a hospital ward and walked about among the men. And then he went over to this dying young officer and stooped down, kissed his forehead and said, "Lieutenant, you've got to get well for me." And the nurses around said they heard a whispered word, "Mr. President, I'll do it." And he did!

Another time they went into his office where he sat gazing out the window over the grassy sward below, and said, "Mr. President, you seem very serious today."

"Yes," he said, "today is 'butcher day.' They're going to shoot a lot of boys today in the army for retreating under fire or doing something else in wartime. I don't blame those boys; they weren't cowards. Their legs did it." Along with his tears he said, "I'm going over the list, and I'm going to save every one that I can."

That's why we love Lincoln, not just because he freed the slaves or saved the Union, but because he had a big heart. But even he had a limit. It is said that somebody once came onto the White House lawn and Lincoln's wife Mary was running and screaming. The great, tall president was following behind her with a paddle.

"What's going on here?" the person asked.

He said, "She won't obey."

He could get mad, you see. And he could act unkind, but not Jesus. The kindest man ever to draw human breath is Jesus.

A group of literary men was talking about pathos in literature. They were discussing books that moved you to tears. Matthew Arnold said of Burns that his poetry was so poignantly beautiful, piercingly pathetic, that it was hard sometimes to read because it wounds you so deeply. Somebody asked Mr. Dickens what literature he thought had the most pathos. "Oh," he said, "there is no question—the story of the Prodigal Son. There is nothing like it in all literature."

Who wrote that story? God. Who spoke it? The kindest man in all the world. When I'm reading through the Scriptures and I come to that passage, "*A certain man had two sons,*" (Luke 15:11) instinctively I bow my head. Something in me wants to go down in obeisance before the heart that could think up that story.

God is not revolted by our wretchedness. He has no despite of anything that He has made, nor does He disdain the service in the simplest office that to our body belongeth. The Lord will be your Nurse, your Caretaker, your Helper, and He's not revolted by anything about you. He wills that you joy along with Him. The everlasting marvel and the high, overpassing love of God, the irresistible love of God, out of His goodness sees us perfect even though we are not perfect. And He wants us to be glad in Him.

He takes no pleasure in human tears. He came and wept that He might stop up forever the fountain of human tears. He came and bereaved His mother that He might heal all bereavement. He came and lost everything that He might heal the wounds that we have from losing things. And He wants us to take pleasure in Him. Let us put away our doubts and trust Him.

God wants to please you. He is pleased when you are His child, when you're surrendered, when your will is His will and His will is yours, when you are not in rebellion and not seeking your own will. God loves to please His people.

Did you ever see a father bringing gifts to his children? Did you ever see a lover bringing gifts to his bride? He wants to please the people He loves, and the people that love Him. The idea that God must always make you miserable is not a biblical idea at all. Jesus Christ knew God and He suffered from the irritations and persecutions of the world, the bitterness of their polluted hearts. They made it hard for Him. But He was pleased with God and God was pleased with Him.

"*This is my beloved Son, in whom I am well pleased.*" (Matthew 3:17) "*Well done, thou good and faithful servant.*" (Matthew 25:21) God can say that now to His people.

God isn't pleased by your being miserable. He will make you miserable if you won't obey, but if you're surrendered and obedient, the goodness of God has so wrought through Jesus Christ that now He wants to please you. And He wants to answer your prayers so you will be happy in Him. He wants to do that. Let's put away all doubts and trust Him.

Gerhard Tersteegen wrote a song.

> *Midst the darkness storm and sorrow,*
>
> *One bright gleam I see.*
>
> *Well I know that blest tomorrow,*
>
> *Christ will come for me.*

And then he writes six stanzas and the last four lines are these:

> *He and I in that bright glory,*
>
> *One deep joy shall share.*
>
> *Mine to be forever with Him,*
>
> *And His that I am there.*

Did you ever stop to think that God is going to be as pleased to have you with Him in heaven as you are to be there? The goodness and mercy of God, the loving kindness of the Lord—it's wonderful! He can bring us into such a relationship with Him that He can please us without spoiling us. He pleases us, and He's pleased when we're pleased. And when we're pleased with Him, He's pleased.

One common joy we will share: "mine to be forever with Him, and His that I am there." Thank God, thank God! Let us praise the lovingkindness of God forever, for of His goodness there is no end. Amen! Amen!

The Holy Spirit Overlooked

The Comforter, which is the Holy Ghost.
(John 14:26)

The Holy Spirit in the Godhead

You will notice I use interchangeably the words "Spirit" and "Ghost." They mean exactly and precisely the same thing. Our English word "Ghost" comes from the old Anglo-Saxon word "gast" and means "Spirit." The phrase "Holy Ghost" comes from the old Elizabethan and pre-Elizabethan English the "holy gast." Therefore, it makes no difference, which I say, I mean the same thing.

Let me start by reminding you that about a century ago the theological liberals in our country committed a great blunder. That blunder took the form of neglecting or denying the deity of Jesus. They either did not talk about it at all, or else they explained the deity of Jesus away, and neglected to mention His lordship over the Church.

It leaves them nothing but an imperfect Christ whose death was a mere martyrdom and whose resurrection is a myth. They who follow a merely human savior follow no savior at all, but an ideal only, and one furthermore that can do no more than mock their weaknesses and sins. So-called Christian leaders shrug this off, but their responsibility toward the souls of their flocks cannot be dismissed with a shrug. God will yet bring them to account for the injury they have done to the plain people who trusted them as spiritual guides.

But however culpable the act of the liberal in denying the Godhood of Christ, we who pride ourselves on our orthodoxy must not allow our indignation to blind us to our own shortcomings. Certainly, this is no time for self-congratulations, for we too have in recent years committed a costly blunder in religion, a blunder paralleling closely that of the liberal.

Our blunder (or shall we frankly say our sin?) has been to neglect the doctrine of the Spirit to a point where we virtually deny Him

His place in the Godhead. This denial has not been by open doctrinal statement, for we have clung closely enough to the biblical position wherever our credal pronouncements are concerned. Our formal creed is sound. The breakdown is in our *working* creed.

This is not a trifling distinction. A doctrine has practical value only as far as it is prominent in our thoughts and makes a difference in our lives. By this test the doctrine of the Holy Spirit as held by evangelical Christians today has almost no practical value at all.

In most Christian churches, the Spirit is quite entirely overlooked. Whether He is present or absent makes no real difference to anyone. Brief reference is made to Him in the doxology and the benediction. Further than that He might as well not exist. So completely do we ignore Him that it is only by courtesy that we can be called Trinitarian.

The Christian doctrine of the Trinity boldly declares the equality of the Three Persons and the right of the Holy Spirit to be worshiped and glorified. Anything less than this is something less than Trinitarianism.

Our neglect of the doctrine of the blessed Third Person has had and is having serious consequences. For doctrine is dynamite. It must have emphasis sufficiently sharp to detonate it before its power is released. Failing this it may lie quiescent in the back of our minds for the whole of our lives without effect.

The doctrine of the Spirit is buried dynamite. Its power awaits discovery and use by the Church. The power of the Spirit will not be given to any mincing asset to pneumatological truth. The Holy Spirit cares not at all whether we write Him into our creeds in the back of our hymnals; He awaits our *emphasis*. When He gets into the thinking of the teachers He will get into the expectation of the hearers. When the Holy Spirit ceases to be incidental and again becomes fundamental, the power of the Spirit will be asserted once more among the people called Christians.

The idea of the Spirit held by the average church member is so vague as to be nearly non-existent. When he thinks of the matter at all he is likely to try to imagine a nebulous substance like a wisp of invisible smoke which is said to be present in churches and to hover over good people when they are dying.

Frankly he does not believe in any such thing, but he wants to believe something, and not feeling up to the task of examining the whole truth in the light of Scripture he compromises by holding belief in the Spirit as far out from the center of his life as possible, letting it make no difference in anything that touches him practically. This describes a surprisingly large number of earnest persons who are sincerely trying to be Christians.

Now, how should we think of the Spirit? A full answer might well run to a dozen volumes. We can at best only point to the "gracious unction from above" and hope that the reader's own desire may provide the necessary stimulus to urge him on to know the blessed Third Person for himself.

The Lordship of the Spirit

This failure to honor the Holy Spirit has resulted in much desolation within the Church. For one, the fellowship of the Church has degenerated into a social fellowship with a mild religious flavor.

For me, either I want God or I do not want anything at all to do with religion. I could never get interested in some old maid's social club, with a little bit of Christianity thrown in to give it respectability. Either I want it all or I do not want any. I want God or I am perfectly happy to go out and be something else.

I think the Lord had something like that in mind when He said, "*I know thy works, that thou art neither cold nor hot: I would thou wert cold or hot.*" (Revelation 3:15 KJV)

Another result of the failure to honor the Holy Ghost is that so many non-spiritual, un-spiritual and anti-spiritual features have been brought into the church. The average church could not run on a hymnbook and a Bible. The church started out with a Bible and then developed a hymnbook, and for years, that was enough. Now, some people could not serve God without at least one vanload of equipment to keep them happy.

All this attraction to win people and keep them coming may be fine, it may be elevated, it may be cheap, it may be degrading, it may be coarse, it may be artistic—but it all depends on who is running the show. Because the Holy Spirit is not the center of attraction, and the Lord is not the one in charge, we must bring in all sorts of anti-scriptural and un-scriptural claptrap to keep the people happy and keep them coming.

The horrible part is not so much that this is true, but that it needs to be at all. The great woe is not the presence of religious toys and trifles, but the necessity for them because the presence of the Eternal Spirit is not in our midst. The tragedy and woe of the hour is trying to make up for His absence by doing these things to keep our own spirits up.

I mentioned once in a sermon in Chicago that some churches are so completely out of the hands of God, if the Holy Ghost withdrew from them, they would not find it out for three months. Afterward I received a telephone call from a woman.

The voice on the phone said, "Mr. Tozer, I am not a member of your church; I am a member of a church on the north side."

If you know anything about that great city, you know that being on the north side is like being in another state.

She said, "I was down to your church last night and heard you say that there are churches where, if the Holy Spirit should desert them, they'd never find it out. Mr. Tozer, I want you to know that's what has happened in our church."

Her voice was tender and broken, there was no criticism, and I tried to console her.

"Well, maybe," I said, "it's just that He is grieved, or maybe He's not given His place."

"No," she said, "it's past that, Mr. Tozer. We have so consistently rejected Him in our church that He is gone; He is no longer here."

Now, I doubt whether she is right. I do not believe the Spirit of God ever leaves the church completely, but He can, like the Savior who was asleep in the hinder part of the ship, go to sleep and not make Himself known and let us get along without Him for years.

To fully understand this, I must ask you to shake your head real hard and wake up some of those cells that have not had a good workout since you got out of college. I'm going to ask you to think with me about something that is a little bit off the beaten track.

The Nature of Spirit

Let me pose a simple question. What is the Holy Spirit?

A great deal can be learned about the Holy Spirit from the word *spirit* itself. In the first place, spirit is another mode of being than matter. You can pick a thing up and bounce it around; that is matter. You and I are composed of matter. That head you have is matter. That is only one mode of existence, but there is another, and that is spirit.

The difference between matter and spirit is that matter possesses weight, size, color and extension in space. It can be measured and weighed and has form. But the Holy Spirit is not material, therefore He does not have weight or dimension or shape or extension in space. These qualities belong to matter and can have no application to spirit. Yet spirit has true being and is objectively real.

If this is hard to visualize, just pass it up, for it is at best but a clumsy attempt of the mind to grasp that which is above the mind's powers. And no harm is done if, in our thinking about the Spirit, we are forced by the limitations of our intellects to clothe Him in the familiar habiliments of material form.

One quality belonging to the Holy Spirit, of great interest and importance to every seeking heart, is penetrability. He can penetrate matter and things and all substances. Your spirit, for instance, dwells in your body somewhere, and it penetrates your body without hurting the body. It is in there penetrating because it is another form.

When Jesus had risen from the dead and was no more mere matter, He came into a locked room through the wall somehow, and managed to penetrate and get into that room without unlocking the door. He could not have done that prior to his death, but He did it afterward.

Spirit, then, is another kind of substance. It is different from material things and can penetrate personality. Your spirit can penetrate your personality. One personality can penetrate another personality. The Holy Spirit can penetrate your personality and your spirit. He can invade the human heart and make room for Himself without expelling anything essentially human. The integrity of the human personality remains unimpaired. Only moral evil is forced to withdraw.

The Bible refers to this in 1 Corinthians, *"For what man knoweth the things of a man, save the spirit of man which is in him? Even so the things of God knoweth no man, but the Spirit of God."* (1 Corinthians 2:11 KJV)

Therefore, the Spirit of God can penetrate the spirit of man.

The metaphysical problem involved here can no more be avoided than it can be solved. How can one personality enter another? The candid reply would be simply that we do not know, but a near approach to an understanding may be made by a simple analogy borrowed from the old devotional writers of several hundred years ago.

We place a piece of iron in a fire and blow up the coals. At first, we have two distinct substances, iron and fire. When we insert the iron in the fire, we achieve the penetration of the iron and we have not only the iron in the fire but the fire in the iron as well. They are two distinct substances, but they have co-mingled and interpenetrated to a point where the two have become one.

In some such manner does the Holy Spirit penetrate our spirits. In the whole experience we remain our very selves. There is no destruction of substance. Each remains a separate being as before; the difference is that now the Spirit penetrates and fills our personalities and we are *experientially one with God.*

Let me mention what the Holy Spirit is *not.*

The Holy Spirit is not enthusiasm. Some people get enthusiasm and imagine it is the Holy Spirit. They become worked up over a song thinking it is Spirit-anointed worship. And they imagine that is the Spirit. Enthusiasm is not the Holy Spirit, because those same people go out and live just like the world. The Holy Spirit never enters a man and then lets him live like the world. You can be sure of that.

Incidentally, that is the reason most people do not want to be filled with the Holy Spirit; they want to live the way they want to live and have the Holy Spirit as a bit of something extra, as you might have a diamond stickpin or something very beautiful on your clothing. They want the Holy Ghost to be something added, but the Holy Spirit will not be an addition. The Holy Spirit must be Lord or He will not come at all.

The Holy Spirit is not courage, or energy, or the personification of all good qualities, like Jack Frost is the personification of cold weather and Santa Claus the personification of wanting to give someone a tie.

The Holy Spirit is not a personification of anything, but the Holy Spirit is a person just the same as you are a person. He has all the qualities of a person. The Holy Spirit has substance but not material substance. He has individuality. He is one being and not another. He has will and He has intelligence and He has feeling and He has knowledge, sympathy, and the ability to love and see and think and hear and speak and desire and grieve and rejoice.

And Jesus said about the Holy Spirit, *"But when the Comforter is come, whom I will send unto you from the Father, even the Spirit of truth, which proceedeth from the Father, He shall testify of Me."* (John 15:26 KJV)

I have said the Holy Spirit is spirit and not matter. He is personality, He is individuality. He has intelligence, love, memory and can communicate with you. He can love you and therefore can be grieved when you grieve Him. He can be quenched, as any friend can be if you turn on Him, of course He will be hushed into hurt silence, because you have wounded Him. Therefore, we can wound the Holy Spirit.

Personal Experience

If I read aright the record of Christian experience through the years, those who most enjoyed the power of the Spirit have had the least to say about Him by way of attempted definition.

The Bible saints who walked in the Spirit never tried to explain Him. In post-biblical times many who were filled and possessed by the Spirit were by the limitations of their literary gifts prevented from telling us much about Him. They had no gifts for self-analysis but lived from within in uncritical simplicity.

To them, the Spirit was One to be loved and fellowshipped the same as the Lord Jesus Himself. They would have been lost completely in any metaphysical discussion of the nature of the Spirit, but they had no trouble in claiming the power of the Spirit for holy living and fruitful service.

This is as it should be. Personal experience must always be first in real life. The most important thing is that we experience reality by the shortest and most direct method. A child may eat nutritious food without knowing anything about the chemistry or dietetics. A country boy may know the delights of pure love while never having heard of Sigmund Freud or Havelock Ellis. Knowledge by acquaintance is always better than mere knowledge by description, and the first does not presuppose the second nor require it.

In religion more than in any other field of human experience a sharp distinction must always be made between *knowing about* and *knowing*. The distinction is the same as between knowing about food and actually eating it. A man can die of starvation knowing all about bread, and a man can remain spiritually dead while knowing all the historic facts of Christianity.

"This is life eternal, that they might know thee the only true God, and Jesus Christ, whom thou hast sent." (John 17:3)

We have but to introduce one extra word into this verse to see how vast is the difference between knowing about and knowing. "This is life eternal, that they might know *about* thee the only true God, and Jesus Christ, whom thou hast sent." That one word makes all the difference between life and death, for it goes to the very root of the verse and changes its theology radically and vitally.

For all this we would not underestimate the importance of mere knowing about. Its value lies in its ability to rouse us to desire to know in actual experience. Thus, knowledge by description may lead on to knowledge by acquaintance. *May* lead on, I say, but does not necessarily do so. Thus we dare not conclude that because we learn about the Spirit we for that reason actually know Him. Knowing Him comes only by a personal encounter with the Holy Spirit Himself.

The Holy Spirit, Present

The Holy Spirit is God

Now, that is what He is. But who is the Holy Spirit?

Consider the testimony of the Church down through the years. The historic church has consistently given witness that the Holy Spirit is God. Those who attended some of the denominational churches are familiar with the Nicene Creed, quoted every so often. The historic Church when she formulated her "rule of faith" boldly wrote into her confession her belief in the Godhood of the Holy Ghost. The Apostles' Creed witnesses to faith in the Father and in the Son and in the Holy Ghost and makes no difference between the three. The fathers who composed the Nicene Creed testified in a passage of great beauty to their faith in the deity of the Spirit:

> And I believe in the Holy Ghost, the Lord and Giver of life, who proceedeth from the Father and the Son; who with the Father and the Son together is worshiped and glorified.

The Arian controversy of the fourth century compelled the fathers to state their beliefs with greater clarity than before. Among the important writings which appeared at the time is the Athanasian Creed. Who composed it matters little to us now. It was written as an attempt to state in as few words as possible what the Bible teaches about the nature of God; and this it has done with a comprehensiveness and precision hardly matched anywhere in the literature of the world. Here are a few quotations bearing on the deity of the Holy Ghost:

> There is one Person of the Father, another of the Son: and another of the Holy Ghost.

> But the Godhead of the Father, of the Son, and of the Holy Ghost, is all one: the Glory equal, the Majesty co-eternal.

> And in this Trinity none is afore, or after other: none is greater, or less than another;

> But the whole three Persons are co-eternal together: and co-equal.

So that in all things, as is aforesaid: the Unity in Trinity, and Trinity in Unity is to be worshiped.

The Church has freely acknowledged the Godhead of the Spirit in her sacred hymnody, and in her inspired song she has worshiped Him with joyous abandon. Some of our hymns to the Spirit have become so familiar that we tend to miss their true meaning by the very circumstances of their familiarity. Such a hymn is the wondrous "Holy Ghost, with Light Divine"; another is the more recent "Breathe on Me, Breath of God"; and there are many others. They have been sung so often by persons who have had no experiential knowledge of their content that for the most of us they have become almost meaningless.

In the poetical works of Frederick Faber, I have found a hymn to the Holy Spirit which I would rank among the finest ever written, but so far as I know it has not been set to music, or if it has, it is not sung today in any church with which I am acquainted. Could the reason be that it embodies a personal experience of the Holy Spirit so deep, so intimate, so fiery hot that it corresponds to nothing in the hearts of the worshipers in present-day evangelicalism? I quote three stanzas:

Fountain of Love! Thyself true God!

Who through eternal days

From Father and from Son hast flowed

In uncreated ways!

I dread Thee, Unbegotten Love!

True God! sole Fount of Grace!

And now before Thy blessed throne

My sinful self abase.

O Light! O Love! O very God

I dare no longer gaze

Upon Thy wondrous attributes

And their mysterious ways.

These lines have everything to make a great hymn—sound theology, smooth structure, lyric beauty, high compression of profound ideas and a full charge of lofty religious feeling. Yet they are in complete neglect. I believe that a mighty resurgence of the Spirit's power among us will open again wells of hymnody long forgotten. For song can never bring the Holy Spirit, but the Holy Spirit does invariably bring song.

There is another creed called the Athanasian Creed. That came into being when a man stood up and said that Jesus was a good man and a great man, but He was not God. He was not divine, nor was He the second person of the Trinity. In response to this heresy, another man responded by declaring the Bible teaches that Jesus is God. All kinds of controversy erupted around this doctrine.

Finally, some came to Athanasia and said, "Athanasia, the whole world is against you on this." He said, "All right, then I'm against the whole world." He did not mind having them against him, he stood his ground.

This came to a peak at a great gathering at Nice, and out of it came the Athanasian Creed. The Church Fathers got together, and they hammered out what the Bible had to say about the Three Persons of the Trinity. Most of us are so busy reading religious fiction that we never get around to it. Therefore, I thought it might be beneficial if I took you back about 1,300 years and listened to our Fathers tell about who God is.

THE ATHANASIAN CREED

Whosoever will be saved, before all things it is necessary that he hold the catholic [i.e., universal, Christian] faith. Which faith except every one do keep whole and undefiled, without doubt he shall perish everlastingly. And the catholic faith is this, that we worship one God in Trinity, and Trinity in Unity; Neither confounding the Persons, nor dividing the Substance. For there is one Person of the Father, another of the Son, and another of the Holy Ghost. But the Godhead of the Father, of the Son, and of the Holy Ghost is all one: the glory equal, the majesty coeternal. Such as the Father is, such is the Son, and such is the Holy Ghost. The Father uncreated, the Son uncreated, and the Holy Ghost uncreated. The Father incomprehensible, the Son incomprehensible, and the Holy Ghost incomprehensible. The

Father eternal, the Son eternal, and the Holy Ghost eternal. And yet they are not three Eternals, but one Eternal. As there are not three Uncreated nor three Incomprehensibles, but one Uncreated and one Incomprehensible. So likewise the Father is almighty, the Son almighty, and the Holy Ghost almighty. And yet they are not three Almighties, but one Almighty. So the Father is God, the Son is God, and the Holy Ghost is God. And yet they are not three Gods, but one God. So likewise the Father is Lord, the Son Lord, and the Holy Ghost Lord. And yet not three Lords, but one Lord. For like as we are compelled by the Christian verity to acknowledge every Person by Himself to be God and Lord, So are we forbidden by the catholic religion to say, There be three Gods, or three Lords.

The Father is made of none: neither created nor begotten. The Son is of the Father alone; not made, nor created, but begotten. The Holy Ghost is of the Father and of the Son: neither made, nor created, nor begotten, but proceeding. So there is one Father, not three Fathers; one Son, not three Sons; one Holy Ghost, not three Holy Ghosts. And in this Trinity none is before or after another; none is greater or less than another; But the whole Three Persons are coeternal together, and coequal: so that in all things, as is aforesaid, the Unity in Trinity and the Trinity in Unity is to be worshiped. He, therefore, that will be saved must thus think of the Trinity.

Furthermore, it is necessary to everlasting salvation that he also believes faithfully the incarnation of our Lord Jesus Christ. For the right faith is that we believe and confess that our Lord Jesus Christ, the Son of God, is God and Man; God of the Substance of the Father, begotten before the worlds; and Man of the substance of His mother, born in the world; Perfect God and perfect Man, of a reasonable soul and human flesh subsisting. Equal to the Father as touching His Godhead, and inferior to the Father as touching His manhood; Who, although He be God and Man, yet He is not two, but one Christ: One, not by conversion of the Godhead into flesh, but by taking the manhood into God; One altogether; not by confusion of Substance, but by unity of Person. For as the reasonable soul and flesh is one man, so God and Man is one Christ; Who suffered for our salvation; descended into hell, rose again the third day from the dead; He ascended into heaven; He sitteth on the right hand of the Father, God Almighty; from whence He shall come to judge the quick and the dead. At Whose coming all men shall rise again with their bodies, and shall give an account of their own works. And they that have done good shall go into life everlasting; and they that have done evil, into everlasting fire.

This is the catholic faith; which except a man believe faithfully and firmly, he cannot be saved.

I do not know what something like that does to you, but that is just like a chicken dinner to my soul, to know this has come down the years and is what our Fathers believed. When that company of Christians met and declared this kind of thing, some had their tongues pulled out, some had their ears burned off, some had their arms torn off and some lost a leg all because they stood for this thing; that Jesus is Lord to the glory of God the Father. The Romans persecuted them under Diocletian, Caligula, and the rest of them. These men were martyrs who hadn't quite died, but who were maimed horribly. Old saints of God and scholars, who knew the truth, came together, wrote this and gave it to the world and for the ages. And I thank God on my knees for them.

The Scripture on the Spirit

Not only does the historic church say that the Holy Spirit is God, but the Scriptures say that the Holy Spirit is God.

If the Church said it and the Scripture did not say it, I would reject it. I would not believe an Archangel if he came to me with a wingspread of twelve feet shining like an atom bomb just at the moment it goes off, if he could not give me chapter and verse. I want to know it is here in the book.

I am not a traditionalist. Anybody comes to me and says this is traditional; I will say, "all right, interesting, if true, but, is it true? Give me chapter and verse." All tradition must bow in reverence before the clear testimony of God's Word.

What I want to know is, were these old brethren, when they said all this, were they telling the truth? Well, listen to what the scriptures have to say.

The Bible declares that He is God. He is not God's messenger only; *He is God.* He is God in contact with His creatures, doing in them and among them a saving and renewing work. All that God is, the Spirit is declared to be. The Spirit of God is one with and equal to God just as the spirit of a man is equal to and one with the man. This is so fully taught in the Scriptures that we may without loss to the argument omit the formality of proof texts. The most casual reader will have discovered it for himself.

Every quality belonging to Almighty God is freely attributed to Him.

For instance, the 139th Psalm says, "*Whither shall I go from thy spirit? or whither shall I flee from thy presence?*" (Psalms 139:7) That is omnipresence. Not even the devil is omnipresent. Only God can claim omnipresence. The Psalmist attributed omnipresence to the Holy Spirit.

Then in Job, He is given the power to create. "*By his spirit he hath garnished the heavens; his hand hath formed the crooked serpent.*" (Job 26:13)

And he said, "*The spirit of God hath made me, and the breath of the Almighty hath given me life,*" (Job 33:4) There we have the breath, the "gast," the "ghost," the Spirit of the Almighty has given me life. Therefore, the Holy Spirit here is said to be Creator. He issues commands, "Thus saith the Spirit," and only God can do that.

The Persons of the Godhead never work separately. We dare not think of them in such a way as to "divide the substance." Every act of God is done by all three Persons. God is never anywhere present in one Person without the other two. He cannot divide Himself. Where the Spirit is, there also is the Father and the Son. "We will come unto him, and make our abode with him" (John 14:23). For the accomplishment of some specific work one Person may for the time be more prominent than the others are, but never is He alone. God is altogether present wherever He is present at all.

Then there is the baptismal formula. "I baptize you in the name of the Father, and of the Son, and of the Holy Ghost."

There is the benediction, "The grace of Christ, and the love of God, and the communion of the Holy Ghost."

This may be a little shocking, but I want to ask you; if the Spirit of God was not God, but something less, if He was a man or an angel, or something else; if He just was not God as some people say, how would it sound if I introduced the name of someone else? The archangel, Gabriel, for instance.

Suppose I said, "I baptize you in the name of the Father and the Son and Saint Paul." Wouldn't that be a shocking, horrible thing? If I said,

"I baptize you in the name of the Father and the Son and the Virgin Mary."

Wouldn't that be a horrible thing? For you cannot attribute deity to Saint Paul. You cannot attribute deity to the Virgin, although we honor her, because she was the mother of our Lord. The Mother of our Lord's body, but not the mother of the Lord's deity. For His deity had been before the foundation of the world.

"In the beginning was the Word, and the Word was with God, and the Word was God ... and all things were made by him; and without him was not anything made that was made."

And the holy Lord, whom she bore, had made the very atoms that composed the body of His mother. Suppose we introduced her there, or introduced Gabriel the Archangel there? And we would say, "The grace of our Lord Jesus Christ, the love of God and the communion of the Archangel Gabriel."

Everyone would run for the door. They would say, "There's heresy in that church." It would be a horrible thing to introduce an archangel or a man in where the Holy Spirit belongs, never, never, my brother. The Holy Spirit is God, and the most important thing here tonight is that the Holy Spirit is present. There is unseen deity present.

He is Like Christ

To the reverent question, "What is God like?" a proper answer will always be, "He is like Christ." For Christ is God, and the Man who walked among men in Palestine was God acting like Himself in the familiar situation where His incarnation placed Him. To the question, "What is the Spirit like?" the answer must always be, "He is like Christ." For the Spirit is the essence of the Father and the Son. As they are, so is He. As we feel toward Christ and toward our Father who art in heaven, so should we feel toward the Spirit of the Father and the Son.

The Holy Spirit is the Spirit of life and light and love. In His uncreated nature, He is a boundless sea of fire, flowing, moving ever, performing as He moves the eternal purposes of God. Toward nature He performs one sort of work, toward the world another, and toward the Church still another. And every act of His accords with the will of the Triune God. Never does He act on impulse nor move after a quick or arbitrary decision. Since He is the Spirit of the Father He feels toward His people exactly as the Father feels, so there need be on our part no sense of strangeness in His presence. He will always act like Jesus, toward sinners in compassion, toward saints in warm affection, toward human suffering in tenderest pity and love.

It is time for us to repent, for our transgressions against the blessed Third Person have been many and much aggravated. We have bitterly mistreated Him in the house of His friends. We have crucified Him in His own temple as they crucified the Eternal Son on the hill above Jerusalem.

And the nails we used were not of iron, but of finer and more precious stuff of which human life is made. Out of our hearts we took the refined metals of will and feeling and thought, and from them we fashioned the nails of suspicion and rebellion and neglect. By unworthy thoughts about Him and unfriendly attitudes toward Him we grieved and quenched Him days without end.

The truest and most acceptable repentance is to reverse the acts and attitudes of which we repent. A thousand years of remorse over a wrong act would not please God as much as a change of conduct and a reformed life. *"Let the wicked forsake his way, and the unrighteous man his thoughts: and let him return unto the LORD, and he will have mercy upon him; and to our God, for he will abundantly pardon."* (Isaiah 55:7)

We can best repent our neglect by neglecting Him no more. Let us begin to think of Him as One to be worshiped and obeyed. Let us throw open every door and invite Him in. Let us surrender to Him every room in the temple of our hearts and insist that He enter and occupy as Lord and Master within His own dwelling. And let us remember that He is drawn to the sweet name of Jesus as bees are drawn to the fragrance of clover. Where Christ is honored the Spirit is sure to feel welcome; where Christ is glorified He will move about freely, pleased and at home.

He is Present in Our Midst

I cannot bring Him here. I can only tell you that He is here. That is all. I can tell you that He is present in our midst, a knowing, feeling personality. He knows how you are reacting to what I am saying. He knows why you came. He knows what you are going to say as soon as you get out on the sidewalk. He knows how you are thinking now. He knows your "uprising and your down sitting" and understands your thoughts afar off.

And you cannot hide from Him. He is present in our midst. "I will send another Comforter, to you and He will abide with you." Therefore, He is here among us. We meet as Christians, and there is an invisible presence among our assembly. We cannot see Him but we know He is present.

He is indivisible from the Father and the Son. In addition, He is all God and exercises all the rights of God, and He merits all worship, all love and all obedience.

That is who the Holy Spirit is. And here is a beautiful thing about the Holy Spirit: being the Spirit of Jesus you will find Him exactly like Jesus. Many people have been frightened by people claiming to be filled with the Spirit and acting anyway else but like the Spirit. Some people say that when they are filled with the Spirit, they are very stern, harsh and abusive. Others do weird things and say that is the Holy Spirit. The Holy Spirit is exactly like Jesus, just as Jesus is exactly like the Father. "He that hath seen me hath seen the Father," said Jesus. "I will send you another Comforter, and he will take the things of mine and show them unto you." In other words Jesus is saying, "He will demonstrate me to you."

What does the Holy Spirit think of babies? Well, what did Jesus think of babies? He thought of babies just what the Father did. And the Father must think wonderfully well of babies because the Son took a baby in His arms, put His hand on his little bald head and said, "God bless you."

Maybe theologians do not know why He did it, but I think I do. Nothing is sweeter and softer in the entire world than the top of a little baby's head. Jesus put His hand on that little soft head and blessed it in the name of His Father. The Holy Spirit is the Spirit of Jesus. What does the Spirit think of babies, then? The Spirit thinks of babies exactly what Jesus did.

What does the Spirit think of sick people? Well, what did Jesus think of sick people?

What does the Spirit think of sinful people? What did Jesus think of the woman, dragged into His presence, taken in adultery? The Spirit feels exactly the way Jesus feels about everything. He is the Spirit of Jesus and He acts exactly the way Jesus acts. If Christ Jesus our Lord was to walk down our church aisle and we could think Him here, no person would run from Him. Nobody. Mothers brought their babies, the sick came, the weary came, the tired came, the dispossessed came. Everybody came, because He was the most magnetic person that ever lived. Even old Fredrick Nietzsche—that nihilistic German philosopher that brought on world wars I and II, and laid the foundation for the Nazis—That old, ungodly fellow said, "I love Jesus, but I hate that man Paul." He could not take Paul but he loved Jesus.

You will not find anybody saying very much against Jesus personally, because Jesus was the most winsome, the most loving, the most kindly, the tenderest, the most beautiful character that ever lived in the entire world. And you know what He was? He was demonstrating the Spirit. That is the way the Spirit is.

The Holy Spirit is friendly. We try to make Him something else but friendly, but He is friendly. Because He is friendly, He can be grieved. We can grieve Him by ignoring Him, by resisting Him, by doubting Him or by sinning against Him. We grieve Him by refusing to obey Him, by turning our backs on Him.

Keep in mind, there must be love present before there can be grief. Let me give you an example.

Suppose you had a seventeen-year-old son who began to go bad, who got to that age where he wanted to take things into his own hand. Suppose he joined up with some boy you did not know, some stranger from another part of town, and they got into trouble. You were called down to the police station and there sat your boy, and another boy you had never seen, in handcuffs. You know how you would feel about it. You would be sorry for the other boy, but you did not know him; but with your own boy, your grief would penetrate your heart like a sword. For only love can grieve. If those two boys were sent off to prison, you might pity the boy you did not know, but you would grieve over the boy you did know.

The mother can grieve because she loves. If you do not love, you cannot grieve. Therefore, when the scripture says, "Grieve not the Holy Spirit of God," it is telling us that He loves us so much that when we insult Him, He is grieved. When we ignore Him, He is grieved; when we resist Him, He is grieved; when we doubt Him, He is grieved.

In like manner, we can please Him by obeying and believing. When we please Him, He responds to us just as a pleased father responds, just as a pleased mother responds. He will respond to us because He is pleased, because He loves us.

If we were to increase our attendance until there wasn't a place to put them, if we were to get $10,000 or $20,000 given to us, if we were to have anything that men want and love and put value on without the Holy Spirit, you might as well have nothing at all. For *"This is the word of the LORD unto Zerubbabel, saying, Not by might, nor by power, but by my Spirit, saith the LORD of hosts."* (Zechariah 4:6) Not by the eloquence of a man, not by good music, not by good preaching, but it is by the Spirit that God works His mighty work.

We had better throw ourselves back on God, for there will be a day when we will have nothing but God.

What is the Spirit? Who is the Spirit? How do we know who the Spirit is? We know by the Scriptures. We know because the Church Fathers knew what the Scriptures said. Unless He is feelingly in our midst, unless He is consciously in our midst, He might as well be somewhere else.

It is possible to run a church without the Holy Spirit, which is a terrible thing. You organize it. You get a board, a pastor, a choir, a ladies' aid society and a Sunday school, and you get all organized. I believe in organization. I am not against it; I am for it. You get organized, and you get a pastor to turn the crank, and that is all there is to it. The Holy Ghost can leave, and the pastor goes on turning the crank, and nobody finds it out for five years. Oh, what a horrible tragedy to the Church of Christ.

But we do not have to have it that way. This kind of preaching is going to do one of two things. There is going to be a reaction from it, or there is going to be an eager seeking. I'm praying and believing the latter will be the case. I believe that there will be an eager seeking for better things than that we now have.

God's Word to the church today is the restoration of the Spirit to His rightful place in the Church, and in your life is, by all means, the most important that could possibly take place.

The Need for Regeneration

Moses my servant is dead; now therefore arise, go over this Jordan, thou, and all this people, unto the land which I do give to them, even to the children of Israel. Every place that the sole of your foot shall tread upon, that have I given unto you, as I said unto Moses.

JOSHUA 1:2-3

You can always test the quality of religious teaching by the enthusiastic reception it receives from unsaved men. If the natural man receives it enthusiastically, it is not of the Spirit of God. Paul says plainly that the natural man cannot know spiritual things. To him, spiritual things are plain foolishness (see 1 Cor. 2:14).

There is a type of religious teaching understood, received by and perfectly logical to the natural man. But the natural man does not know that which is of the Spirit of God. He does not have the faculty to receive it.

The natural man is of this world. He may be in perfect health and have an IQ of 180. He may be as handsome as a Greek statue or, if a woman, a perfect example of fine womanhood. Or he might be a perfect example of the young American. The natural man, though he is in this state, is unblessed and out of grace.

Contrary to the natural man is the spiritual man. This is the Christian who is mature in his faith, who is led, taught and controlled by the Holy Spirit, and to whom the Spirit of God can speak.

Then there is the carnal man. The carnal man is the immature Christian. He is no longer a natural man, for he has been renewed by the grace of God and is in a state of grace, but he is not spiritual. He is halfway in between the two. He has been regenerated but is not advancing in his spiritual life. He is not influenced or led by the Holy Spirit but rather is controlled by his lower nature.

Of the three types, it is the spiritual man who is living the crucified life. He is indwelt, led, taught, influenced and controlled by the Holy Spirit.

A New Birth

The Old Testament prototype of the natural man—those who are not in a state of grace—was Israel in Egypt. Four hundred years the Israelites had been in Egypt, and a major part of that time they had been in bondage to Pharaoh. Then came Moses who, through blood and atonement and power, led the children of Israel out of Egypt with the Red Sea closing between Israel and Egypt. That corresponded to the new birth.

Regeneration, or rebirth, makes the natural man a Christian, which takes him out of nature and puts him in a state of grace. Israel came out of Egypt and went across the sea, and the sea closed behind them and the enemy died. Israel for the first time in 400 years was a free nation, redeemed by blood and by power.

This is like the Christian who for all of his lifetime has been subject to bondages of various kinds—chains and shackles and manacles have been upon his spirit. Now, through the blood of the Lamb, the power of the Spirit, he is brought out of Egypt, and the Red Sea closes after him. We used to sing the hymn "I've Turned My Back upon the World" by Elisha A Hoffman:

I've turned my back upon the world

With all its idle pleasures,

And set my heart on better things,

On higher, holier treasures;

No more its glitter and its glare,

And vanity shall blind me;

I've crossed the separating line,

And left the world behind me.

These words describe exactly what happened to Israel in the land of Canaan. It was God's benevolent intention that the natural man in bondage in Egypt should come out of Egypt and make an 11-day journey to the holy land offered to Abraham by God in covenant. The holy land—variously called the Promised Land, the land of promise, and Canaan—was to be the homeland of Israel.

Israel was not only to be out of Egypt but also to be in the holy land, their spiritual homeland. God brought them out so that He might bring them in. This point has been lost in our teaching today. God brings us out, not that we may be out, but that we may be brought in.

God saves a criminal not so that he might tell about it once a year for the next 40 years, but so that he might become a saint. God takes him out of his bondage that He might lead that person into the Promised Land. And the farther in the man goes, the less he will have to say about where he used to be. It is not the mark of spirituality when I talk at length about what I used to be. Israel wanted to forget what she used to be and remembered only occasionally to thank God for her deliverance.

Today, we magnify what we used to be and write books to tell the world about it. Paul said, *"Those things ought not even to be mentioned among the people of God."* (see Eph. 5:12) They are not even to be mentioned in conversation. God brought you out, but He does not leave you in limbo. He brought you out so that He might bring you in, and that was the will of God.

After God brought Israel out of Egypt, He showed them, after an 11-day march, the Promised Land. The enemy could have been driven out, and they could have had the holy land of promise God had given to them centuries before. They would not be stealing it. They would be occupying it as their proper possession. God, who owned it, had given it to Abraham and his seed after him. Abraham's seed had been driven out and into Egypt. God was now bringing Israel back to put them in the land. They were not to be usurpers—not to take the land—but to occupy the land, which was properly theirs by a gift of the One who owned it: God.

Metaphorically, God brought the Israelites out of sin so that He might bring them into the spiritual life. The Israelites' march was a God-blessed, God-hovered-over and Shekinah-enlightened journey straight through to the Holy Land. When they arrived in the land of promise from which Abraham had come centuries before, they were to be spiritual men. They represent an Old Testament prototype of the spiritual man.

The Natural Man

If you are a natural man, no matter how learned, how talented, how handsome or how desirable you are, you do not know a thing about God and you do not know a thing about the spiritual life. You do not have the faculties to know it.

If a man who is stone deaf sits reading while a Mozart Symphony is playing, you would not blame him because he would rather read than listen to the music. He does not have the ability to enjoy the music. The ability you have in you to listen to the symphony is dead in him.

Or if you were in an art gallery looking at paintings and there was a man completely blind sitting on the bench, you would not say, "Why is that Philistine just sitting there? Why doesn't he get up and look at the paintings?" He does not have the ability to look at paintings. The ability you have to look at paintings is dead in him.

No matter who you are or how learned or religious you are, if you have not been regenerated, renewed, made over, brought to the light by the quickening of the Holy Spirit, you cannot know God. You cannot know spiritual things at all; you can only know the history of spiritual things. Any enthusiasm you have for religion is but an illusion.

The Spiritual Man

Paul says that we Christians who are quickened to life—who are God's children, who are not in the state of nature anymore but in a state of grace—but who continue without progress year after year, wander spiritually instead of moving straight ahead. Sometimes we may get a little closer to Egypt than to the Holy Land; then we again get a little closer to the Holy Land; then back to Egypt. So we swing on our pendulum, back and forth, occasionally looking over the sea and remembering that we used to be slaves.

Then we go to a prayer meeting or some revival, put out our arms, and we move so close to the Holy Land that we can almost touch it. But we are not going to either place. We are not going back into the world, and we are not going to push on into the spiritual life. So back and forth we go, swinging between the old world we came from and the new world where we ought to be.

To continue without progress year after year is to develop a sort of chronic heart disease. Your heart becomes harder and harder as time passes. The best time to plunge into the deeper spiritual life is when you are a young Christian and have enthusiasm and can form deep-seated habits.

If I were to try to learn Japanese at my age, it would almost be hopeless. I could learn to read and write it. But I could never speak it well enough to be understood, because I have been around too long and my tongue and lips and palate have been too used to only having to form English words. All the little twists, turns and slurs of the English tongue fit my mouth. The older I get, the harder it is for me to learn a new language. However, a young person can pick it up and rattle it off in no time flat. The younger you are, the easier it is to learn and speak a new language because over time, habits have a tendency to harden you.

The Carnal Man

Now, what about the carnal man? The carnal man is the immature Christian who does not go on or advance. He is slowed in His spiritual development and is not influenced or controlled by the Holy Spirit but rather by his lower nature.

When Israel came to Kadesh-Barnea after marching a little while in the direction of the Promised Land, they stopped (see Num. 13–14). Moses said to them, in effect, "We're about to enter into the land that has been the object of your hope since God brought you out of Egypt."

Israel responded, "We're a little afraid. So send up twelve men to spy on the land." So Moses sent twelve men to examine the land and report back to determine whether they could take it or not. When the spies came back, all of them reported that it was an exceedingly good land. There was water there. To people in that country, water amounted to riches untold. It was more valuable than silver and gold and diamonds. So to report that this was an exceedingly good land in which there was much water was equivalent to saying that it was a sort of paradise.

They found grapes so large that it took two men to carry one branch between them. They found dates, which would have been our equivalent of sugar, candy, preserves, marmalade jelly and sodas. Everybody has his sweet tooth, and they had their dates. Figs and dates were probably the sweetest part of their diet. And there were pomegranates. Pomegranates are berries but are near enough to citrus fruit to have been classified as it. They are literally packed with vitamins. They would be well worth having.

Then there was milk and honey. When the Bible says *"a land flowing with milk and honey,"* this is not careless language (Exod. 3:8). There were a great many bees in the land. There was so much honey that the trees could not hold it all, so it literally dripped down on great rocks. And there was abundant milk from sheep and goats. This land was so different from Egypt, the land they had come from only a little while before.

Now, after ten of these twelve men came back and reported what the country was like, they nevertheless said, "We advise you not to go up into the land because although it is an exceedingly good land with lots of water, grapes, figs, pomegranates, milk and honey, the people are large and strong. There are giants there and their cities are great and walled up to heaven."

A land with brooks of water, grapes, figs, pomegranates, milk and honey does not sound to me as if it were being eaten up by its giant inhabitants. Besides that, the spies had not stayed long enough to watch the inhabitants eat up anything. The ten men were simply frightened and filled with unbelief and advised against going on.

"Let's stay here in the wilderness," was their advice. "We're free of Egypt, thank God, and are not slaves anymore. We are in the wilderness, and while it isn't the best, we will settle for it rather than go up against those giants in that wonderful promised homeland."

Then Caleb and Joshua stepped to the head of the line and said to Moses, "We are ready to go in. Pay no attention to these pessimists. We can easily take the land, and there will be bread for us. The land belongs to us, our father's God gave it to us—gave it to Abraham, our father—and it's ours. Let's go take it."

Caleb and Joshua told of the rich advantages in the land and were unwilling to allow the large strong giants in the walled cities to keep them out.

All the teaching today about the Church being the perfect democracy and about how there should be no leaders is just plain poppycock with nothing in the Old or New Testaments to support it. Twelve leaders were sent to spy out the land, and the people were more or less dependent on what those leaders said, just as you and I are similarly dependent in this democracy upon our leaders in Washington to a large extent. And in the Church of Christ, it is the same.

The people heard the unfavorable report of the ten men; that is, the majority report. Caleb and Joshua gave the minority report, but they were only two. The people wept and fell down in front of their tent doors, wishing they had not come out of Egypt. They complained to Moses and said, "Would to God we were back in Egypt."

All the Israelites could see was walled cities and giants. They could not see grapes or goats with their great utters dripping with milk or trees drooling sweet honey down onto the grass. They could not see the rolling grasslands and the brooks and rivers. All they could see were the giants in the land. They forgot that God said, "Go up and I'll give it to you." So they said, "You'll kill our poor women. You'll kill our children."

This is always the unspiritual man's argument: "I've got to think about my family. I've got a family after all, brother, and God wants us to be wise, and I can't push this too far. I can't become too spiritual because I've got to think about my family. I can't subject my wife and children to difficulties. I can't lay burdens on them."

Always pleasing their wives and family, such a man forgets that the best heritage a husband can leave his family is the memory that he was a good man. A spiritual woman also faces stumbling blocks. Her family may fight her with hot language, scold her with sarcastic speech, oppose her and make her feel like an idiot. However, a spiritual woman will walk quietly away, sadder but wiser, and will admit that the best heritage she can leave her family is that she was a good woman.

Had these Israelites only believed, they could have taken all their wives and families into the Holy Land within a few hours. They would have had all that land. Instead, for 40 years, they wandered in the desert. They had been so afraid that those wives and children were going to be killed if they went into that land that they ended up walking for 40 years, wandering round and round and round in the desert. Now swinging back near to Egypt where they had been, now a wide swing close to the Promised Land where they should be. Back again to Egypt where they were not, then around again, then by the loop again near to where they ought to be.

They wandered for 40 years until those children were grown to middle age and those women were dead. Forty years of it because the men had whimpered and said, "We can't go. It would cost us too much. We can't mistreat our families. We have to be with our families on Sunday nights and Wednesday nights and all during the missionary convention. We have to be with our families. We can't take a chance of our children becoming juvenile delinquents."

The best way for a husband to save his family from delinquency is to show them an example of a man who loves God uncompromisingly. A man who seeks to be spiritual, even though it costs him his blood. A man who doesn't listen to the devil's ruse: "You give more than you should to the Lord's work already, and if you seek to become a spiritual man, you will harm your family."

Israel wandered in the desert for 40 years by God's judgment. God said, "*Doubtless ye shall not come into the land.*" (Num. 14:30) Their fear of death and their doubts and complaining displeased God because the people brought "a slander to the land" (Num. 14:36)

Every man who stands in the shadows and slanders the deeper spiritual life is slandering the sunshine. Every man who refuses to enter into the holy life is in the wilderness, slandering the homeland of the soul. For 40 years, Israel wandered aimlessly about. God was with them. He did not destroy them; rather, He let them die one at a time. Occasionally, He would punish them, but He did not destroy them as a nation.

Spiritual Failures

I refuse to be discouraged about anything, but it gives me a heavy heart to walk among Christians who have wandered for forty long years in the wilderness, not going back to sin but not going on into the holy life. Wandering in an aimless circle, sometimes a little warmer, sometimes a little colder, sometimes a little holier and sometimes very unholy, but never going on. Habits have been acquired and are hard to break, and it makes it almost certain that they will live and die spiritual failures. To me this is a terrible thing.

A man decides to be a lawyer and spends years studying law and finally puts out his shingle. He soon finds something in his temperament that makes it impossible for him to make good as a lawyer. He is a complete failure. He is 50 years old, was admitted to the bar when he was 30, and 20 years later, he has not been able to make a living as a lawyer. As a lawyer, he is a failure.

A businessman buys a business and tries to operate it. He does everything that he knows how to do but just cannot make it go. Year after year the ledger shows red, and he is not making a profit. He borrows what he can, has a little spirit and a little hope, but that spirit and hope die and he goes broke. Finally, he sells out, hopelessly in debt, and is left a failure in the business world.

A woman is educated to be a teacher but just cannot get along with the other teachers. Something in her constitution or temperament will not allow her to get along with children or young people. So after being shuttled from one school to another, she finally gives up, goes somewhere and takes a job running a stapling machine. She just cannot teach and is a failure in the education world.

I have known ministers who thought they were called to preach. They prayed and studied and learned Greek and Hebrew, but somehow, they just could not make the public want to listen to them. They just couldn't do it. They were failures in the congregational world.

It is possible to be a Christian and yet be a failure. This is the same as Israel in the desert, wandering around. The Israelites were God's people, protected and fed, but they were failures. They were not where God meant them to be. They compromised. They were halfway between where they used to be and where they ought to be. And that describes many of the Lord's people. They live and die spiritual failures.

I am glad God is good and kind. Failures can crawl into God's arms, relax and say, "Father, I made a mess of it. I'm a spiritual failure. I haven't been out doing evil things exactly, but here I am, Father, and I'm old and ready to go and I'm a failure."

Our kind and gracious heavenly Father will not say to that person, "Depart from me—I never knew you," because that person has believed and does believe in Jesus Christ. The individual has simply been a failure all of his life. He is ready for death and ready for heaven. I wonder if that is what Paul, the man of God, meant when he said:

[No] other foundation can [any] man lay than that is laid, which is Jesus Christ. Now if any man build upon this foundation gold, silver, precious stones, wood, hay, stubble; every man's work shall be made manifest: for the day shall declare it, because it shall be revealed by fire; and the fire shall try every man's work of what sort it is. If any man's work abide which he hath built thereupon, he should receive a reward. If any man's work shall be burned, he shall suffer loss: but he himself shall be saved; yet so as by fire. (1 Cor. 3:11-15)

I think that's what it means, all right. We ought to be the kind of Christian that cannot only save our souls but also save our lives. When Lot left Sodom, he had nothing but the garments on his back. Thank God, he got out. But how much better it would have been if he had said farewell at the gate and had camels loaded with his goods. He could have gone out with his head up, chin out, saying good riddance to old Sodom. How much better he could have marched away from there with his family. And when he settled in a new place, he could have had "an abundant entrance" (see 2 Pet. 1:11).

Thank God, *you* are going to make it. But do you want to make it in the way you have been acting lately? Wandering, roaming aimlessly? When there is a place where Jesus will pour "the oil of gladness" on our heads, a place sweeter than any other in the entire world, the blood-bought mercy seat (Ps. 45:7; Heb. 1:9)? It is the will of God that you should enter the holy of holies, live under the shadow of the mercy seat, and go out from there and always come back to be renewed and recharged and re-fed. It is the will of God that you live by the mercy seat, living a separated, clean, holy, sacrificial life—a life of continual spiritual difference. Wouldn't that be better than the way you are doing it now?

We're Marching to Zion

Isaac Watts (1674–1748)

> *Come, we that love the Lord,*
>
> *And let our joys be known;*
>
> *Join in a song with sweet accord,*

Join in a song with sweet accord

And thus surround the throne,

And thus surround the throne.

We're marching to Zion,

Beautiful, beautiful Zion;

We're marching upward to Zion,

The beautiful city of God.

Let those refuse to sing

Who never knew our God;

But children of the heavenly King,

But children of the heavenly King

May speak their joys abroad,

May speak their joys abroad.

The hill of Zion yields

A thousand sacred sweets

Before we reach the heavenly fields,

Before we reach the heavenly fields,

Or walk the golden streets,

Or walk the golden streets.

Then let our songs abound,

And every tear be dry;

We're marching through Emmanuel's ground,

We're marching through Emmanuel's ground,

To fairer worlds on high,

To fairer worlds on high.

Holy Spirit's Work in Redemption

Infusion of Divine Power

The Christian Scriptures, particularly the gospel of John, contain two truths that appear to stand opposed to each other. One is that whosoever will may come to Christ. The other is that before anyone can come there must have been a previous work done in his heart by the sovereign operation of God. The notion that just anybody, at any time, regardless of conditions, can start from religious scratch, without the Spirit's help, and believe savingly on Christ by a sudden decision of the will, is wholly contrary to the teachings of the Bible.

God's invitation to men is broad but not unqualified. The word "whosoever" throws the door open wide, indeed, but the church in recent years has carried the gospel invitation far beyond its proper bounds and turned it into something more human and less divine than that found in the sacred Scriptures.

All three persons of the Godhead had part in redemption, though the Son paid the redemptive price to the Father through the Spirit.

Becoming a Christian is not just nodding to a few truths and then saying, "I accept Jesus." It is infusing into your life the divine power, the same power that raised Jesus from the dead. This is the tremendous work of the Holy Spirit to bring you into the divine world of redemption.

Coming into the presence of God is not something accomplished in human strength, as I pointed out, but only through the power of the Holy Spirit within me, enabling me to penetrate deep into the heart of God. The deeper into the heart of God I go, the more the enemy will oppose me, but the more God will draw me. The enemy may be strong, but his strength is limited, whereas God's grace has no limit. *"Greater is he that is in you, than he that is in the world."* (1 John 4:4)

Through the light of nature man's moral reason may be enlightened, but the deeper mysteries of God remain hidden to him until he has received illumination from above.

But the natural man receiveth not the things of the Spirit of God: for they are foolishness unto him: neither can he know them, because they are spiritually discerned. (1 Corinthians 2:14)

When the Spirit illuminates the heart, then a part of the man sees which never saw before; a part of him knows which never knew before, and that with a kind of knowing which the most acute thinker cannot imitate. He knows now in a deep and authoritative way, and what he knows needs no reasoned proof. His experience of knowing is above reason, immediate, perfectly convincing and inwardly satisfying.

Human Intellect Insufficient

John answered and said, A man can receive nothing, except it be given him from heaven.

(John 3:27)

Here in a brief sentence is the hope and despair of mankind. "A man can receive nothing." From the context we know that John is speaking of spiritual truth. He is telling us that there is a kind of truth which can never be grasped by the intellect, for the intellect exists for the apprehension of ideas, and this truth consists not in ideas but in life. Divine truth is of the nature of spirit and for that reason can be received only by spiritual revelation. "Except it be given him from heaven."

This was no new doctrine which John here set forth, but an advance rather upon truth already taught in the Old Testament. The prophet Isaiah, for instance, has this passage.

My thoughts are not your thoughts, neither are your ways my ways, saith the LORD. For as the heavens are higher than the earth, so are my ways higher than your ways, and my thoughts than your thoughts. (Isaiah 55:8-9)

Perhaps this had meant to its readers no more than that God's thoughts, while similar to ours, were loftier, and His ways as high above ours as would befit the ways of One whose wisdom is infinite and whose power is without bounds.

Now John says plainly enough that God's thoughts are not only greater than ours quantitatively by qualitatively wholly different from ours. God's thoughts belong to the world of spirit, and man's to the world of intellect. While spirit can embrace intellect, the human intellect can never comprehend spirit. Man's thoughts cannot cross over into God's.

"How unsearchable are his judgements, and his ways past finding out!" (Romans 11:33)

God made man in His own image and placed within him an organ by means of which he could know spiritual things. When man sinned, that organ died. "Dead in sin" is a description not of the body nor yet of the intellect, but of the organ of God-knowledge within the human soul. Now men are forced to depend upon another and inferior organ and one furthermore which is wholly inadequate to the purpose. I mean, of course, the mind as the seat of his powers of reason and understanding.

Man by reason cannot know God; he can only know about God. Through the light of reason certain important facts about God may be discovered. Because that which may be known of God is manifest in them; for God hath showed it unto them. *For the invisible things of him from the creation of the world are clearly seen, being understood by the things that are made, even his eternal power and Godhead; so that they are without excuse.* (Romans 1:19-20)

"A man can receive nothing." That is the burden of the Bible. Whatever men may think of human reason, God takes a low view of it. *"Where is the wise? where is the scribe? where is the disputer of this world? hath not God made foolish the wisdom of this world?"* (1 Corinthians 1:20)

Man's reason is a fine instrument and useful within its field. It is a gift of God and God does not hesitate to appeal to it, as when He cries to Israel, *"Come now, and let us reason together."* (Isaiah 1:18) The inability of human reason as an organ of divine knowledge arises not from its own weakness but from its unfittedness for the task by its own nature. It was not given as an organ by which to know God.

The doctrine of the inability of the human mind and the need for divine illumination is so fully developed in the New Testament that it is nothing short of astonishing that we should have gone so far astray from the whole thing. Fundamentalism has stood aloof from the liberal in self-conscious superiority and has on its own part fallen into error, the error of textualism, which is simply orthodoxy without the Holy Ghost. Everywhere among conservatives we find persons who are Bible-taught but not Spirit-taught. They conceive truth to be something which they can grasp with the mind. If a man holds to the fundamentals of the Christian faith he is thought to possess divine truth.

But it does not follow. There is no truth apart from the Spirit. The most brilliant intellect may be imbecilic when confronted with the mysteries of God. For a man to understand revealed truth requires an act of God equal to the original act which inspired the text.

"Except it be given him from heaven." Here is the other side of the truth; here is hope for all, for these words do certainly mean that there is such a thing as a gift of knowing, a gift that comes from heaven. Christ taught His disciples to expect the coming of the Spirit of Truth who would teach them all things. He explained Peter's knowledge of His Saviorhood as being a direct revelation from the Father in heaven. And in one of His prayers He said:

I thank thee, O Father, Lord of heaven and earth, because thou hast hid these things from the wise and prudent, and hast revealed them unto babes. (Matthew 11:25)

By "wise and prudent" our Lord meant not Greek philosophers but Jewish Bible students and teachers of the Law.

This basic idea, the inability of human reason as an instrument of God-knowledge, was fully developed in the epistles of Paul. The apostle frankly rules out every natural faculty as instruments for discovering divine truth and throws us back helpless upon the inworking Spirit.

Eye hath not seen, nor ear heard, neither hath entered into the heart of man, the things which God hath prepared for them that love him. But God hath revealed them unto us by his Spirit; for the Spirit searcheth all things, yea, the deep things of God. For what man knoweth the things of a man, save the spirit of man which is in him? even so the things of God knoweth no man, but the Spirit of God. Now we have received, not the spirit of the world, but the spirit which is of God, that we might know the things that are freely given to us of God. (1 Corinthians 2:9-12)

The passage just quoted is taken from Paul's first epistle to the Corinthians and is not lifted out of context nor placed in a setting which would tend to distort its meaning. Indeed, it expresses the very essence of Paul's spiritual philosophy and fully accords with the rest of the epistle, and I might add, with the rest of Paul's writings as we have them preserved in the New Testament. That type of theological rationalism which is so popular today would have been wholly foreign to the mind of the great apostle. He had no faith in man's ability to comprehend truth apart from the direct illumination of the Holy Ghost.

I have just now used the word *rationalism* and I must either retract it or justify its use in association with orthodoxy. The latter I think I shall have no trouble doing. For the textualism of our times is based upon the same premise as the old-line rationalism, that is, the belief that the human mind is the supreme authority in the judgment of truth. Or otherwise stated, it is confidence in the ability of the human mind to do that which the Bible declares it was never created to do and consequently is wholly incapable of doing. Philosophical rationalism is honest enough to reject the Bible flatly. Theological rationalism rejects it while pretending to accept it and in so doing puts out its own eyes.

The inward kernel of truth has the same configuration as the outward shell. The mind can grasp the shell but only the Spirit of God can lay hold of the internal essence. Our great error has been that we have trusted to the shell and have believed we were sound in faith because we were able to explain the external shape of truth as found in the letter of the Word.

From this mortal error fundamentalism is slowly dying. We have forgotten that the essence of spiritual truth cannot come to the one who knows the external shell of truth unless there is first a miraculous operation of the Spirit within the heart. Those overtones of religious delight which accompany truth when the Spirit illuminates it are all but missing from the Church today. Those transporting glimpses of the celestial country are few and dim; the fragrance of "Sharon's dewy Rose" is hardly discernible.

Consequently we have been forced to look elsewhere for our delights and we have found them in the dubious artistry of converted opera singers or the tinkling melodies of odd and curious musical arrangements. We have tried to secure spiritual pleasures by working upon fleshly emotions and whipping up synthetic feeling by means wholly carnal. And the total effect has been evil.

In a remarkable sermon on "The True Way of Attaining Divine

Knowledge," John Smith states the truth I am attempting to set forth here.

> Were I indeed to define divinity, I should rather call it a divine life than a divine science; it is something rather to be understood by a spiritual sensation, than by any verbal description.... Divinity is indeed a true efflux from the eternal Light, which like the sunbeams, does not only enlighten, but heat and enliven.... We must not think that we have attained to the right knowledge of truth, when we have broken through the outward shell of words and phrases that house it up....

There is a knowing of Truth as it is in Jesus, as it is in a Christlike nature, as it is in that sweet, mild, humble and loving Spirit of Jesus, which spreads itself like a morning sun upon the souls of good men, full of life and light. It profits little to know Christ Himself after the flesh; but He gives His Spirit to good men that search the deep things of God. There is an inward beauty, life and loveliness in divine Truth, which can be known only when it is digested into life and practice.

Purity of Life Essential

This old divine held that a pure life was absolutely necessary to any real understanding of spiritual truth.

There is an inward sweetness and deliciousness in divine truth, which no sensual mind can taste or relish: this is that "natural" man that savors not the things of God.... Divinity is not so much perceived by a subtle wit as by a purified sense.

Twelve hundred years before these words were uttered, Athanasius had written a profound treatise called, "The Incarnation of the Word of God." In this treatise he boldly attacked the difficult problems inherent in the doctrine of the incarnation. The whole thing is a remarkable demonstration of pure reason engaged with divine revelation. He makes a great case for the deity of Christ and, for all who believe the Bible, settles the matter for all time. Yet so little does he trust the human mind to comprehend divine mysteries that he closed his great work with a strong warning against a mere intellectual understanding of spiritual truth. His words should be printed in large type and tacked on the desk of every pastor and theological student in the world:

But for the searching of the Scriptures and true knowledge of them, an honorable life is needed, and a pure soul, and that virtue which is according to Christ; so that the intellect guiding its path by it may be able to attain what it desires, and to comprehend it, in so far as it is accessible to human nature to learn concerning the Word of God. For without a pure mind and a modeling of the life after the saints, a man could not possibly comprehend the words of the saints…. He that would comprehend the mind of those who speak of God needs begin by washing and cleansing his soul.

The old Jewish believers of pre-Christian times who gave us the (to modern Protestants little-known) books, the Wisdom of Solomon and Ecclesiasticus, believed that it is impossible for an impure heart to know divine truth.

For into a malicious soul wisdom will not enter; nor dwell in the body that is subject unto sin. For the holy spirit of discipline will flee deceit, and remove from thoughts that are without understanding, and will not abide when unrighteousness cometh in.

These books, along with our familiar Book of Proverbs, teach that true spiritual knowledge is the result of a visitation of heavenly wisdom, a kind of baptism of the Spirit of Truth which comes to God-fearing men. This wisdom is always associated with righteousness and humility and is never found apart from godliness and true holiness of life.

Conservative Christians in this day are stumbling over this truth. We need to re-examine the whole thing. We need to learn that truth consists not in correct doctrine, but in correct doctrine plus the inward enlightenment of the Holy Spirit. We must declare again the mystery of wisdom from above. A re-preachment of this vital truth could result in a fresh breath from God upon a stale and suffocating orthodoxy.

Errors In the Church Today

Inspiration

Two aspects of the Bible that are critical to coming into God's presence are revelation and inspiration. In the volumes of Christian testimony that have come down through the centuries, there are two words that occur frequently: one is "inspiration," and the other is "revelation."

When we say "inspiration," meaning that the Scripture is inspired or given by inspiration, we mean that in its original signature, that is, as originally given, the Holy Spirit inspired the Bible to be written. What we have was put down at the order of the Holy Spirit. That is what we mean by inspiration.

We humans do not have the ability to apprehend divine things, but it also states that the ability can be given us from heaven. It is quite plain in the scriptural revelation that spiritual things are hidden by a veil, and by nature, a human does not have the ability to comprehend and get hold of them. He comes up against a blank wall. He takes doctrine and texts and proofs and creeds and theology, and lays them up like a wall—but he cannot find the gate! He stands in the darkness and all about him is intellectual knowledge of God—but not the knowledge of God, for there is a difference between the intellectual knowledge of God and the Spirit-revealed knowledge.

It is possible to grow up in a church, learn the catechism, and have everything done to us that they do to us, within reason. But after we have done all that, we may not know God at all, because God isn't known by those external things. We are blind, and can't see, because the things of God no man knows but by the Spirit of God.

The Holy Spirit said through the Apostle Paul, "... even so the things of God knoweth no man but by the Spirit of God." God knows Himself, and the Holy Ghost knows God because the Holy Ghost is God, and no man can know God except by the Holy Ghost. Now, for any man to disregard this truth is to entirely shut out spiritual things from his understanding.

How I wish that all of our teachers in the church could understand that the realm of the Spirit is closed to the intellect. It is really not difficult to understand why this is so. You see, the spirit is the agency by which we apprehend divine things, and the human spirit has died—it is dead because of sin.

When I say that the human intellect is not the vehicle by which we apprehend divine things, I am not saying anything very profound. For instance, if there were a symphony being played just now, we wouldn't hear that symphony with our eyes, for God didn't give us our eyes to hear. He gave us our eyes to see. If there were a beautiful sunset, we wouldn't enjoy that with our ears because God didn't give us our ears to hear sunsets. He gave us our ears-to hear music, the voices of our friends, the laughter of children and bird songs. He gave us our eyes to see those things which can be seen. He never confuses the two.

If a man stands up and says the realm of nature—visible nature—cannot be apprehended by the ear, no one gets excited. No one jumps up and says, "That man is a mystic!" He has only said that which is common sense, ordinary scientific fact.

When I say that God did not give us our intellect to apprehend Him, the Divine Being, but that He gave us another means of comprehension, there is nothing profound about that.

But at this point, let's share the Word of God in regard to this concept. Sometimes when we hear a thing explained and then we read the Scripture, it just comes alive for us.

We have read the passage in Isaiah 55:8, 9, "*For my thoughts are not your thoughts, neither are your ways my ways, saith the Lord. For as the heavens are higher than the earth, so are my ways higher than your ways, and my thoughts than your thoughts.*"

Also, in I Corinthians 2:14, "*But the natural man receiveth not the things of the Spirit of God: for they are foolishness unto him: neither can he know them, because they are spiritually discerned.*"

Now hear that. The natural man—that is, the psychic man, the man of mind, the man of intellect—cannot understand nor receive the things of the Spirit of God. They are foolishness to him and he cannot know them because they are spiritually discerned. God gave us spirit to apprehend Himself, and intellect to apprehend theology—there is a difference.

In John 16:12-14, Jesus said, "*I have yet many things to say unto you, but ye cannot bear them now. Howbeit when he, the Spirit of truth, is come, he will guide you into all truth: for he shall not speak of himself; but whatsoever he shall hear, that shall he speak: and he will shew you things to come. He shall glorify me: for he shall receive of mine, and shall shew it unto you.*"

Now that is perfectly plain—the One who reveals God to us, who reveals Christ to us, is the Spirit of God.

In I Corinthians 2:6-9, we have a passage that tells us, "*Howbeit we speak wisdom among them that are perfect: yet not the wisdom of this world, nor of the princes of this world, that come to naught: But we speak the wisdom of God in a mystery, even the hidden wisdom; which God ordained before the world unto our glory: Which none of the princes of this world knew: for had they known it, they would not have crucified the Lord of glory. But as it is written, Eye hath not seen, nor ear heard, neither have entered into the heart of man, the things which God hath prepared for them that love him.*"

It is strange how many times we stop when we should go on; and this is one of the places where people stop when they memorize, and put a full stop after those words "them that love him." We stop there but the Bible doesn't stop there. It has a little conjunctive "but", and it says, "But God hath revealed them unto us by his Spirit." Eye has not seen nor ear heard nor the heart of man understood but God has revealed it by His Spirit. Spiritual things are not apprehended by the eye, nor by the ear, and they are not apprehended even by the intellect. They are revealed by the Spirit, for "... the Spirit searcheth all things, yea, the deep things of God."

Paul uses an illustration in verse 11, saying, "For what man knoweth the things of a man, save the spirit of man which is in him?" Now that's what we call intuition, and that is not a word that we should be afraid of. With the help of God, I don't run from words. I am not afraid of the word "intuition" or "intuit," because that is how I know I am me—and not somebody else!

How do you know that you are you—and not somebody else? If you were to walk up to fourteen other men who looked exactly like you, it wouldn't stun you at all. You would smile and say, "Isn't this an amazing coincidence that fourteen other men look exactly like me." It could be that my wife wouldn't know the difference—but I wouldn't wonder which one I was. You maintain your individuality because of your intuition. You don't run to your old family Bible to find out who you are—you know who you are. If you were left an orphan, you might not know who your parents were, but as far as your individual self is concerned, you know who you are by intuition. And you know that you are alive—you don't reason that you are alive.

Inward Enlightenment

Now, let's apply this to the condition of the church in our day. We forget that there are some things that we cannot get hold of with our minds, so we run around trying to lay hold of them with our minds. The mind is good; God put it there. He gave us our heads, and it was not His intention that our heads would function just as a place to hang a hat. He gave us our heads, and He put brains in our heads, and that faculty we call the intellect has its own work to do. But that work is not the apprehending of divine things—that is of the Holy Ghost.

Let me remind you now that modern orthodoxy has made a great blunder in the erroneous assumption that spiritual truths can be intellectually perceived. There have been far-reaching conditions resulting from this concept—and they are showing in our preaching, our praying, and in our singing, in our activity and in our thinking.

I contend that we are in error to believe that Bible study can remove the veil that keeps us from spiritual perception.

I know that when we go to Bible school, we have to learn theology, Old Testament and New Testament introduction, Old Testament and New Testament synthesis, and on and on it goes. The courses have long names, and I suppose the people who study them think they have something. They could have something provided they have the divine illumination of the Holy Ghost. Until they receive that illumination—that inward enlightenment—they will not have anything because Bible study does not, of itself, lift the veil or penetrate it. The Word does not say "no man knoweth the things of God except the man who studies his Bible." It does say that no man knows the things of God except by the Holy Ghost.

It is the Spirit who wrote the Bible and who must inspire the Bible. Let me quote a little motto—I don't recall where it came from, "To understand a Bible text takes an act of the Holy Spirit equal to the act that inspired the text in the first place."

Personally, I believe that is true. In 2 Timothy 3:16, Paul said, "*All scripture is given by inspiration of God, and is profitable*," and that supports John 3:27, "*A man can receive nothing, except it be given him from heaven.*"

Now, I contend, also, that we are in a state of error when we believe that we can talk each other up and put spiritual things down on a level with man's understanding. We say that a preacher is a salesman—he's out selling the gospel. But don't try to tell me that the methods God uses in winning men are the same as the brush salesman uses in selling a back scratcher. I don't believe it.

The Holy Spirit operates in another realm altogether, and the method of winning a man to God is a divine method and not a human one. Oh, we can make church members. We can get people over on our side, and they can join our class and go to our summer camps. We may have done nothing to them but make proselytes out of them. When the Holy Spirit works in a man, then God does the work, and what God does, according to the Scriptures, is forever.

We imagine that we can handle it by the flesh, and we do handle it by the flesh—the Lord lets us do it. We can hold the creed and not know God in His person at all. We can know the doctrine and not know spiritual things at all.

The fearful consequence is that many people know about God but don't know God Himself. There is a vast difference between knowing about God and knowing God—a vast difference! I can know about your relative—and still not know him in person. If I have never met him, I do not know the touch of his hand, or the look of his eye, or the smile of his face, or the sound of his voice. I only know about him. You can show me his picture and describe him to me, but I still don't know him. I just know about the man.

A scientist knows bugs. He may write books on bees or worms or other bugs of various kinds and yet never know a bug—never! He could never get through to him!

If you have a dog, you can know all about him and his habits, but you will never really know him. He may smile at you, stick out his red tongue and pant. He seems to be intelligent, but he is a dog, and as a human, you have no facility, no organs, no techniques for getting into his dog world. You can comb him, wash him, feed him, trim his ears and you can know him externally, but you never can know your dog in this sense in which we are considering. Your dog can never know you. He can know about you, he can know when you are glad and when you are angry with him. He can know when he has done the right thing or the wrong thing.

Sometimes I think dogs have a conscience almost as good as people, but still the dog dies and never knows the man, because he does not have the capacity given him to comprehend and perceive and understand as a human.

So it is that the human being can know about God, he can know about Christ's dying for him, he can even write songs and books, be the head of religious organizations and hold important church offices— and still never have come to the vital, personal knowledge of God at all. Only by the Holy Ghost can he know God.

Again, it is my contention that as a consequence of this kind of error, we really have two Christs. We have the Christ of history, the Christ of the creeds. On the other hand, there is the Christ whom only the Spirit can reveal.

Now, you can never piece Jesus together out of historic knowledge— it is impossible. It is possible to read your New Testament and still never find the living Christ in it. You may be convinced that He is the Son of God and still never find Him as the living Person He is. Jesus Christ must be revealed by the Holy Ghost—no man knows the things of God but the Holy Ghost.

I would like to make an emphasis here and make it clearly: A revelation of the Holy Spirit in one glorious flash of inward illumination would teach you more of Jesus than five years in a theological seminary—and I believe in the seminary! You can learn about Jesus in the seminary. You can learn a great deal about Him, and we ought to learn everything we can about Him. We ought to read everything we can read about Him, for reading about Him is legitimate and good-a part of Christianity. But the final flassh that introduces your heart to Jesus must be by the illumination of the Holy Spirit Himself, or it isn't done at all.

I am convinced that we only know Jesus Christ as well as the Holy Spirit is pleased to reveal Him unto us, for He cannot be revealed in any other way. Even Paul said, "Now know we Christ no longer after the flesh." The church cannot know Christ except as the Spirit reveals Him.

Bible taught and Spirit-taught

t may shock some readers to suggest that there is a difference between being Bible taught and being Spirit taught. Nevertheless it is so.

It is altogether possible to be instructed in the rudiments of the faith and still have no real understanding of the whole thing. And it is possible to go on to become expert in Bible doctrine and not have spiritual illumination, with the result that a veil remains over the mind, preventing it from apprehending the truth in its spiritual essence.

Most of us are acquainted with churches that teach the Bible to their children from their tenderest years, give them long instruction in the catechism, drill them further in pastor's classes and still never produce in them a living Christianity nor a virile godliness. Their members show no evidence of having passed from death unto life. None of the earmarks of salvation so plainly indicated in the Scriptures are found among them. Their religious lives are correct and reasonably moral, but wholly mechanical and altogether lacking in radiance. They wear their faith as persons in mourning once wore black armbands to show their love and respect for the departed.

Such persons cannot be dismissed as hypocrites. Many of them are pathetically serious about it all. They are simply blind. From lack of the vital Spirit, they are forced to get along with the outward shell of faith, while all the time their deep hearts are starving for spiritual reality and they do not know what is wrong with them.

This difference between the religion of creed and the religion of the Spirit is well set forth by the saintly Thomas in a tender little prayer to his Lord:

The children of Israel in time past said unto Moses, "Speak thou with us, and we will hear: but let not God speak with us, lest we die." Not so, Lord, not so, I beseech Thee; but rather with the prophet Samuel I humbly and earnestly entreat, "Speak, Lord; for Thy servant heareth." Let not Moses speak unto me, nor any of the prophets, but rather do Thou speak, O Lord GOD, the inspirer, enlightener of all the prophets; for Thou alone without them canst perfectly instruct me, but they without Thee can profit nothing. They indeed may utter words, but they cannot give the Spirit. Most beautifully do they speak, but if Thou be silent, they inflame not the heart. They teach the letter, but Thou openest the sense; they bring forth mysteries, but Thou unlockest the heart. ... They cry aloud with words, but Thou impartest understanding to the hearing.

It would be hard to wrap it up better than that. The same thing has been said variously by others; however, the most familiar saying probably is, "The Scriptures, to be understood, must be read with the same Spirit that originally inspired them." No one denies this, but even such a statement will go over the heads of those who hear it unless the Holy Spirit inflames the heart.

The charge often made against us by liberals, that we are "bibliolaters," is probably not true in the same sense as meant by our detractors; but candor and self-analysis will force us to admit that there is often too much truth in their charge. Among religious persons of unquestioned orthodoxy there is sometimes found a dull dependence upon the letter of the text without the faintest understanding of its spirit. That truth is in its essence spiritual must constantly be kept before our minds if we would know the truth indeed. Jesus Christ is Himself the Truth, and He cannot be confined to mere words even though, as we ardently believe, He has Himself inspired the words. That which is spiritual cannot be shut in by ink or fenced in by type and paper. The best a book can do is give us the letter of truth. If we ever receive more than this, it must be by the Holy Spirit who gives it.

The great need of the hour among persons spiritually hungry is twofold: first, to know the Scriptures, apart from which no saving truth will be vouchsafed by our Lord; the second, to be enlightened by the Spirit, apart from whom the Scriptures will not be understood.

Consequences of Wrongful Trust

There are several evil consequences of believing that we can know God with our minds, with our intellectual capacity.

First, the Christian life is conceded to be very much like the natural life—only jollier and cleaner and more fun!

The faith of our fathers has been identified with a number of questionable things. We must admit that one is philosophy, and I think that this modern neo-intellectual movement that is trying to resurrect the church by means of learning is about as far off the track as it is possible to be, for you don't go to philosophy to find out about the Lord Jesus.

Now, the Apostle Paul did happen to be one of the most intellectual men that ever lived. He has been called by some to be one of the six greatest intellects that ever lived, but this man Paul said to the church in Corinth, "And I, brethren, when I came to you, came not with excellency of speech or wisdom but in demonstration of the Spirit and of power."

If you have to be reasoned into Christianity, some wise fellow can reason you out of it! If you come to Christ by a flash of the Holy Ghost so that by intuition you know that you are God's child, you know it by the text but you also know it by the inner light, the inner illumination of the Spirit, and no one can ever reason you out of it.

When I was a young man, I read most of the books on atheism. I had my Bible and a hymnbook and a few other books, including Andrew Murray and Thomas a Kempis, and I got myself educated as well as I could by reading books. I read the philosophy of all of the great minds—and many of those men did not believe in God, you know—and they didn't believe in Christ. I remember reading White's Warfare of Science with Christianity; and if any man can read that and still say he is saved, he isn't saved by his reading, he is-saved by the Holy Ghost within him telling him that he is saved!

Actually, many of those philosophers and thinkers would take away all my "reasons" and reduce me to palpitating ignorance. On the basis of human reason, they would make a man just get down and walk out and toss his Bible on a shelf and say, "There goes another one!"

Do you know what I would do after I would read a chapter or two and find arguments that I could not possibly defeat? I would get down on my knees and with tears I would thank God with joy that no matter what the books said, "I know Thee, my Savior and my Lord!"

I didn't have it in my head—I had it in my heart. There is a great difference, you see. If we have it in our heads, then philosophy may be of some help to us; but if we have it in our hearts, there is not much that philosophy can do except stand aside reverently, hat in hand, and say, "Holy, holy, holy is the Lord God Almighty."

Another of the questionable things is the manner in which we try to call upon science to prove Christianity.

We have just come through one of those long tunnels when the evangelical church was running to science to get some sort of help, not knowing that science has no technique for investigation of all that is divine in Christianity.

The things that science can investigate are not divine and the things that are divine science cannot investigate. Oh, science can make the satellites and the space ships—many wonderful things in the human field—but all of that is really nothing. Christianity is a miracle and a wonder—something out of the heavens—something let down like Peter's sheet, not depending upon the world nor being a part of the world, but something from the throne of God like the waters of Ezekiel's vision.

Science knows nothing about that. It can only stand back, looking it over, and doesn't know what to say. But if we don't have this inner intuition, if we don't have this comprehension of the miraculous, we run to science.

Some of those in this category say they want to believe in miracles. A fellow finds a fish washed up on shore and he gets a tape measure and crawls inside the bony skeleton and measures its gullet. He finds out that it is as broad as the shoulders of a man and he says, "See, Jonah could be swallowed by a great fish!"

Well, I believe the miracles—I believe them all, but I don't believe them because science permits me. I believe them because God wrote them and detailed them in the Bible. If they are there, I believe them!

You may have heard of the two scientists who reported that the story of Balaam's ass speaking to the prophet is false because "the larynx of a donkey could not possibly articulate human speech,"

A thoughtful Scotchman overheard them and he walked up to them and said, "Man, you make a donkey and I'll make him talk."

There you have it, brother. If God can make a donkey, God can make him talk. Christianity stands or falls on Jesus Christ—stands or falls on the illumination of the Holy Ghost.

Peter could have reasoned until the cows came home and still not known anything for sure, but suddenly, when the Holy Ghost came upon him, he jumped up and said, "God has made this man Jesus whom ye crucified Lord and Christ!" He knew that by the Spirit of God.

Still another of the questionable things is the manner in which we patronize human greatness when we have no inward illumination.

A system of literature has grown up around the notion that Christianity may be proven by the fact that great men believe in Christ. If we can just get the story of a politician who believes in Christ, we spread it all over our magazines, "Senator So-and-so believes in Christ." The implication is that if he believes in Christ, then Christ must be all right. When did Jesus Christ have to ride in on the coattail of a senator?

No, no, my brother! Jesus Christ stands alone, unique and supreme, self-validating, and the Holy Ghost declares Him to be God's eternal Son. Let all the presidents and all the kings and queens, the senators, and the lords and ladies of the world, along with the great athletes and great actors—let them kneel at His feet and cry, "Holy, holy, holy is the Lord God Almighty!"

Only the Holy Ghost can do this, my brethren. For that reason, I don't bow down to great men. I bow down to the Great Man, and if you have learned to worship the Son of Man, you won't worship other men.

You see, it is the Holy Spirit or darkness. The Holy Spirit is God's imperative of life. If our faith is to be New Testament faith, if Christ is to be the Christ of God rather than the Christ of intellect, then we must enter in beyond the veil. We have to push in past the veil until the illumination of the Holy Spirit fills our heart and we are learning at the feet of Jesus—not at the feet of men.

Now, consider with me the words of First John 2:27, "*But the anointing which ye have received of him abideth in you, and ye need not that any man teach you: but as the same anointing teacheth you of all things, and is truth, and is no lie, and even as it hath taught you, ye shall abide in him.*"

What does that mean, "... Ye need not that any man teach you but as the same anointing teaches you... " The man who wrote that was a teacher, and we do not rule out the place of the teacher, for one of the gifts of the Spirit is teaching. What it says is that your knowledge of God is not taught to you from without. It is received by an inner anointing, and you don't get your witness from a man—you get your witness from an inner anointing.

Paul said, "*For the preaching of the cross is to them that perish foolishness; but unto us which are saved it is the power of God. For it is written, I will destroy the wisdom of the wise, and will bring to nothing the understanding of the prudent.*"

And, "*... after that in the wisdom of God the world by wisdom knew not God.*" And, "*... because the foolishness of God is wiser than men; and the. weakness of God is stronger than men.*"

Paul also assures us that "*God hath chosen the foolish things of the world to confound the wise; and God hath chosen the weak things of the world to confound the things which are mighty and the base things of the world, and things which are despised, hath God chosen, yea, and the things which are not, to bring to naught things that are: that no flesh should glory in his presence.*"

You see, the Holy Spirit rules out and excludes all Adam's flesh, all human brightness, all that scintillating human personality, human ability and human efficiency. It makes Christianity depend upon a perpetual miracle. The man of God, the true Spirit-filled man of God, is a perpetual miracle. He is someone who is not understood by the people of the world at all. He is a stranger. He has come into the world by the wonder of the new birth and the illumination of the Spirit, and his life is completely different from the world. If you want a scriptural basis for this thought: Paul said in 1 Corinthians 2:15, "*But he that is spiritual judgeth all things, yet he himself is judged of no man.*" The spiritual man has a penetration that judges everything, but he himself cannot be judged by anyone, "*For who hath known the mind of the Lord, that he may instruct him? But we have the mind of Christ.*" That's simple.

Now, what are we going to do with this truth? Are we going to argue about this? Are we just going to say that it was good? Are we going to do something about it? Are we going to open the door of our personality—fling it wide? Oh, we don't have to be afraid—the Holy Spirit is an illuminator. He is light to the inner heart, and He will show us more of God in a moment than we can learn in a lifetime without Him. When He does come, all that we have learned and all that we do learn will have proper place in our total personality and total creed and total thinking.

We won't lose anything by what we have learned. He won't throw out what we have learned if it is truth—He will set it on fire, that's all. He will add fire to the altar.

The blessed Holy Spirit waits to be honored. He will honor Christ as we honor Christ. He waits—and if we will throw open our heart to Him; a new sun will rise on us. I know this by personal experience. If there is anything that God has done through me, it dates back to that solemn, awful, wondrous hour when the Light that never was on land or sea, the Light that lighteth every man that cometh into the world, flashed in on my darkness. It was not my conversion—I had been converted, soundly converted. It was subsequent to conversion. How about you?

Filling of the Spirit

An Absolute Necessity

Be filled with the Spirit.

Ephesians 5:18

That every Christian can be and should be filled with the Holy Spirit would hardly seem to be a matter for debate among Christians. Yet some will argue that the Holy Spirit is not for plain Christians but for ministers and missionaries only. Others hold that the measure of the Spirit received at regeneration is identical with that received by the disciples at Pentecost and any hope of additional fullness after conversion simply rests upon error. A few will express a languid hope that some day they may be filled, and still others will avoid the subject as one about which they know very little and which can only cause embarrassment.

Almost all Christians want to be full of the Spirit. Only a few want to be filled with the Spirit.

But how can a Christian know the fullness of the Spirit unless he has known the experience of being filled?

It would, however, be useless to tell anyone how to be filled with the Spirit unless he first believes that he can be. No one can hope for something he is not convinced is the will of God for him and within the bounds of scriptural provision.

Before the question "How can I be filled?" has any validity the seeker after God must be sure that the experience of being filled is actually possible. The man who is not sure can have no ground of expectation. Where there is no expectation there can be no faith, and where there is no faith the inquiry is meaningless.

The doctrine of the Spirit as it relates to the believer has over the last half century been shrouded in a mist such as lies upon a mountain in stormy weather. A world of confusion has surrounded this truth. The children of God have been taught contrary doctrines from the same texts, warned, threatened and intimidated until they instinctively recoil from every mention of the Bible teaching concerning the Holy Spirit.

This confusion has not come by accident. An enemy has done this. Satan knows that Spiritless evangelicalism is as deadly as Modernism or heresy, and he has done everything in his power to prevent us from enjoying our true Christian heritage.

A church without the Spirit is as helpless as Israel might have been in the wilderness if the fiery cloud had deserted them. The Holy Spirit is our cloud by day and our fire by night. Without Him we only wander aimlessly about the desert.

That is what we today are surely doing. We have divided ourselves into little ragged groups, each one running after a will-o'-the-wisp or firefly in the mistaken notion that we are following the Shekinah. It is not only desirable that the cloudy pillar should begin to glow again. It is imperative.

The Church can have light only as it is full of the Spirit, and it can be full only as the members that compose it are filled individually. Furthermore, no one can be filled until he is convinced that being filled is a part of the total plan of God in redemption; that it is nothing added or extra, nothing strange or queer, but a proper and spiritual operation of God, based upon and growing out of the work of Christ in atonement.

I want here boldly to assert that it is my happy belief that every Christian can have a copious outpouring of the Holy Spirit in a measure far beyond that received at conversion, and I might also say, far beyond that enjoyed by the rank and file of orthodox believers today. It is important that we get this straight, for until doubts are removed faith is impossible. God will not surprise a doubting heart with an effusion of the Holy Spirit, nor will He fill anyone who has doctrinal questions about the possibility of being filled.

To remove doubts and create a confident expectation I recommend a reverent study of the Word of God itself. I am willing to rest my case upon the teachings of the New Testament. If a careful and humble examination of the words of Christ and His apostles does not lead to a belief that we may be filled with the Holy Spirit now, then I see no reason to look elsewhere. For it matters little what this or that religious teacher has said for or against the proposition. If the doctrine is not taught in the Scriptures, then it cannot be supported by any argument, and all exhortations to be filled are valueless.

I shall not here present a case for the affirmative. Let the inquirer examine the evidence for himself, and if he decides that there is no warrant in the New Testament for believing that he can be filled with the Spirit, let him shut this book and save himself the trouble of reading further. What I say from here on is addressed to men and women who have gotten over their questions and are confident that when they meet the conditions they may indeed be filled with the Holy Spirit.

The Power and the Spirit

But ye shall receive power,
after that the Holy Ghost is come upon you.
ACTS 1:8

Some good Christians have misread this text and have assumed that Christ told His disciples that they were to receive the Holy Spirit *and* power, the power to come after the coming of the Spirit. A superficial reading of the King James text might conceivably lead to the conclusion, but the truth is that Christ taught not the coming of the Holy Spirit *as* power; the power and the Spirit are the same.

Our mother tongue is a beautiful and facile instrument, but it can also be a tricky and misleading one. For this reason it must be used with care if we would avoid giving and receiving wrong impressions by its means. Especially is this true when we are speaking of God, for God is wholly unlike anything or anybody in His universe. Our very thoughts of Him as well as our words are in constant danger of going astray.

One example is found in the words, "The power of God." The danger is that we think of "power" as something belonging to God as muscular energy belongs to a man, as something which He *has* and which might be separated from Him and still have existence in itself. We must remember that the "attributes" of God are not component parts of the blessed Godhead nor elements out of which He is composed. A god who could be *composed* would not be God at all but the work of something or someone greater than he, great enough to compose him.

We would then have a synthetic god made out of the pieces we call attributes, and the true God would be another being altogether, One indeed who is above all thought and all conceiving.

The Bible and Christian theology teach that God is an indivisible unity, being what He is in undivided oneness, from whom nothing can be taken and to whom nothing can be added. Mercy, for instance, immutability, eternity—these are but names which we have given to something which God has declared to be true of Himself. All the "of God" expressions in the Bible must be understood to mean not what God has but *what God is* in His undivided and indivisible unity. Even the word "nature" when applied to God should be understood as an accommodation to our human way of looking at things and not as an accurate description of anything true of the mysterious Godhead. God has said, *"I AM THAT I AM,"* (Exodus 3:14) and we can only repeat in reverence, *"O God, Thou art."*

Our Lord before His ascension said to His disciples, *"Tarry ye in the city of Jerusalem, until ye be endued with power from on high."* (Luke 24:49) That word *until* is a time-word; it indicates a point in relation to which everything is either before or after.

So the experience of those disciples could be stated like this. Up to that point they *had not* received the power; at that point they *did* receive the power; after that point they *had* received the power. Such is the plain historic fact.

Power came upon the Church, such power as had never been released into human nature before (with the lone exception of that mighty anointing which came upon Christ at the waters of Jordan). That power, still active in the Church, has enabled her to exist for nearly twenty centuries, even though for all of that time she has remained a highly unpopular minority group among the nations of mankind and has always been surrounded by enemies who would gladly have ended her existence if they could have done so.

"Ye shall receive power." By those words our Lord raised the expectation of His disciples and taught them to look forward to the coming of a supernatural potency into their natures from a source outside of themselves. It was to be something previously unknown to them, but suddenly to come upon them from another world. It was to be nothing less than God Himself entering into them with the purpose of ultimately reproducing His own likeness within them.

Here is the dividing line that separates Christianity from all occultism and from every kind of oriental cult, ancient or modern. These all are built around the same ideas, varying only in minor details, each with its own peculiar set of phrases and apparently vying with each other in vagueness and obscurity. They each advise, "Get in tune with the infinite," or "Wake the giant within you," or "Tune in to your hidden potential" or "Learn to think creatively."

All this may have some fleeting value as a psychological shot in the arm, but its results are not permanent because at its best it builds its hopes upon the fallen nature of man and knows no invasion from above. And whatever may be said in its favor, *it most certainly is not Christianity.*

Christianity takes for granted the absence of any self-help and offers a power which is nothing less than the power of God. This power is to come upon powerless men as a gentle but resist-less invasion from another world, bringing a moral potency infinitely beyond anything that might be stirred up from within. This power is sufficient; no additional help is needed, no auxiliary source of spiritual energy, for it is the Holy Spirit of God come where the weakness lay to supply power and grace to meet the moral need.

Set over against such a mighty provision as this ethical Christianity (if I may be allowed the term) is seen to be no Christianity at all. An infantile copying of Christ's "ideals," a pitiable effort to carry out the teachings of the Sermon on the Mount! All this is but religious child's play and is not the faith of Christ and the New Testament.

"Ye shall receive power." This was and is a unique afflatus, an enduement of supernatural energy affecting every department of the believer's life and remaining with him forever. It is not physical power nor even mental power though it may touch everything both mental and physical in its benign outworking. It is, too, another kind of power than that seen in nature, in the lunar attraction that creates the tides or the angry flash that splits the great oak during a storm.

This power from God operates on another level and affects another department of His wide creation. It is spiritual power. It is the kind of power that God is. It is the ability to achieve spiritual and moral ends. Its long-range result is to produce Godlike character in men and women who were once wholly evil by nature and by choice.

Now how does this power operate? At its purest, it is an unmediated force directly applied by the Spirit of God to the spirit of man. The wrestler achieves his ends by the pressure of his physical body upon the body of his opponent; the teacher by the pressure of ideas upon the mind of the student; the moralist by the pressure of duty upon the conscience of the disciple. So the Holy Spirit performs His blessed work by direct contact with the human spirit.

It would be less than accurate to say that the power of God is always experienced in a direct and unmediated form, for when He so wills the Spirit may use other means as Christ used spittle to heal a blind man. But always the power is above and beyond the means. While the Spirit may use appropriate means to bless a believing man, He never need do so, for they are at best but temporary concessions made to our ignorance and unbelief. Where adequate power is present almost any means will suffice, but where the power is absent not all the means in the world can secure the desired end. The Spirit of God may use a song, a sermon, a good deed, a text or the mystery and majesty of nature, but always the final work will be done by the pressure of the inliving Spirit upon the human heart.

In the light of this it will be seen how empty and meaningless is the average church service today. All the means are in evidence; the one ominous weakness is the absence of the Spirit's power. The form of godliness is there, and often the form is perfected till it is an aesthetic triumph. Music and poetry, art and oratory, symbolic vesture and solemn tones combine to charm the mind of the worshiper, but too often the supernatural afflatus is not there. The power from on high is neither known nor desired by pastor or people. This is nothing less than tragic, and all the more so because it falls within the field of religion where the eternal destinies of men are involved.

To the absence of the Spirit may be traced that vague sense of unreality which almost everywhere invests religion in our times. In the average church service the most real thing is the shadowy unreality of everything. The worshiper sits in a state of suspended thought; a kind of dreamy numbness creeps upon him; he hears words but they do not register; he cannot relate them to anything on his own life-level. He is conscious of having entered a kind of half-world; his mind surrenders itself to a more or less pleasant mood which passes with the benediction, leaving no trace behind.

It does not affect anything in his everyday life. He is aware of no power, no presence, no spiritual reality. There is simply nothing in his experience corresponding to the things which he heard from the pulpit or sang in the hymns.

One meaning of the word "power" is "ability to do." There precisely is the wonder of the Spirit's work in the Church and in the hearts of Christians, His sure ability to make spiritual things real to the soul. This power can go straight to its object with piercing directness; it can diffuse itself through the mind like an infinitely fine volatile essence securing ends above and beyond the limits of the intellect. Reality is its subject matter, reality in heaven and upon earth. It does not create objects which are not there but reveals objects already present and hidden from the soul.

In actual human experience this is likely to be first felt in a heightened sense of the presence of Christ. He is felt to be a real Person and to be intimately, ravishingly near. Then all other spiritual objects begin to stand out clearly before the mind. Grace, forgiveness, cleansing take on a form of almost bodily clearness. Prayer loses its unmeaning quality and becomes a sweet conversation with Someone actually there. Love for God and for the children of God takes possession of the soul. We feel ourselves near to heaven and it is now the earth and the world that begin to seem un-real. We know them now for what they are, realities indeed, but like stage scenery here for one brief hour and soon to pass away. The world to come takes on a hard outline before our minds and begins to invite our interest and our devotion.

Then the whole life changes to suit the new reality and the change is permanent. Slight fluctuations there may be like the rise and dip of the line on a graph, but the established direction is upward and the ground taken is held.

This is not all, but it will give a fair idea of what is meant when the New Testament speaks of *power,* and perhaps by contrast we may learn how little of the power we enjoy.

I think there can be no doubt that the need above all other needs in the Church of God at this moment is the power of the Holy Spirit. More education, better organization, finer equipment, more advanced methods—all are unavailing. It is like bringing a better respirator after the patient is dead. Good as these are they can never give life. "*It is the spirit that quickeneth.*" (John 6:63) Good as they are they can never bring power. "*Power belongeth unto God.*" (Psalm 62:11)

Protestantism is on the wrong road when it tries to win merely by means of a "united front." It is not organizational unity we need most; the great need is power. The headstones in the cemetery present a united front, but they stand mute and helpless while the world passes by.

I suppose my suggestion will not receive much serious attention, but I should like to suggest that we Bible-believing Christians announce a moratorium on religious activity and set our house in order preparatory to the coming of an afflatus from above. So carnal is the body of Christians which composes the conservative wing of the Church, so shockingly irreverent are our public services in some quarters, so degraded are our religious tastes in still others that the need for power could scarcely have been greater at any time in history.

I believe we should profit immensely were we to declare a period of silence and self-examination during which each one of us searched his own heart and sought to meet every condition for a real baptism of power from on high.

We may be sure of one thing, that for our deep trouble there is no cure apart from a visitation, yes, an *invasion* of power from above. Only the Spirit Himself can show us what is wrong with us and only the Spirit can prescribe the cure. Only the Spirit can save us from the numbing unreality of Spiritless Christianity. Only the Spirit can show us the Father and the Son. Only the inworking of the Spirit's power can discover to us the solemn majesty and the heart ravishing mystery of the Triune God.

How to Be Filled

The Desire for Filling

Before a man can be filled with the Spirit *he must be sure he wants to be.* And let this be taken seriously. Many Christians want to be filled, but their desire is a vague romantic kind of thing hardly worthy to be called desire. They have almost no knowledge of what it will cost them to realize it.

The inquirer must be sure to the point of conviction. He must believe that the whole thing is normal and right. He must believe that God wills that he be anointed with a horn of fresh oil beyond and in addition to all the ten thousand blessings he may already have received from the good hand of God.

Until he is so convinced, I recommend that he take time out to fast and pray and meditate upon the Scriptures. Faith comes from the Word of God. Suggestion, exhortation or the psychological effect of the testimony of others who may have been filled will not suffice.

Unless he is persuaded from the Scriptures, he should not press the matter nor allow himself to fall victim to the emotional manipulators intent upon forcing the issue. God is wonderfully patient and understanding and will wait for the slow heart to catch up with the truth. In the meantime, the seeker should be calm and confident. In due time God will lead him through the Jordan. Let him not break loose and run ahead. Too many have done so, only to bring disaster upon their Christian lives.

After a man is convinced that he can be filled with the Spirit he must desire to be.

Let us imagine that we are talking to an inquirer, some eager young Christian, let us say, who has sought us out to learn about the Spirit-filled life. As gently as possible, considering the pointed nature of the questions, we would probe his soul somewhat as follows:

"Are you sure you want to be filled with a Spirit who, though He is like Jesus in His gentleness and love, will nevertheless demand to be

Lord of your life? Are you willing to let your personality to be taken over by another, even if that other be the Spirit of God Himself? If the Spirit takes charge of your life, He will expect unquestioning obedience in everything. He will not tolerate in you the self-sins even though they are permitted and excused by most Christians. By the self-sins I mean self-love, self-pity, self-seeking, self-confidence, self-righteousness, self-aggrandizement, self-defense.

"You will find the Spirit to be in sharp opposition to the easy ways of the world and of the mixed multitude within the precincts of religion. He will be jealous over you for good. He will take the direction of your life away from you. He will reserve the right to test you, to discipline you, to chasten you for your soul's sake. He may strip you of those borderline pleasures which other Christians enjoy but which are to you a source of refined evil.

"Through it all He will enfold you in a love so vast, so mighty, so all-embracing, so wondrous that your very losses will seem like gains and your small pains like pleasures. Yet the flesh will whimper under His yoke and cry out against it as a burden too great to bear. And you will be permitted to enjoy the solemn privilege of suffering to 'fill up that which is behind of the afflictions of Christ' in your flesh for His body's sake, which is the Church (Colossians 1:24). Now, with the conditions before you, do you still want to be filled with Holy Spirit?"

If this appears severe, let us remember that the way of the cross is never easy. The shine and glamour accompanying popular religious movements is as false as the sheen on the wings of the angel of darkness when he for a moment transforms himself into an angel of light. The spiritual timidity that fears to show the cross in its true character is not on any grounds to be excused. It can result only in disappointment and tragedy at last.

All-Consuming

Before we can be filled with the Spirit *the desire to be filled must be all-consuming.* It must be for the time the biggest thing in life, so acute, so intrusive as to crowd out everything else. The degree of fullness in any life accords perfectly with the intensity of true desire. We have as much of God as we actually want.

One great hindrance to the Spirit-filled life is the theology of complacency so widely accepted among gospel Christians today. According to this view, acute desire is evidence of unbelief and proof of lack of knowledge of the Scriptures. A sufficient refutation of this position is afforded by the Word of God itself and by the fact that it always fails to produce real saintliness among those who hold it.

Unless you can answer an eager "Yes" to these questions you do not want to be filled. You may want the thrill or the victory or the power, but you do not really want to be filled with the Spirit. Your desire is little more than a feeble wish and is not pure enough to please God, Who demands all or nothing.

Again I ask: Are you sure you need to be filled with the Spirit? Tens of thousands of Christians, laymen, preachers, missionaries, manage to get on somehow without having had a clear experience of being filled. That Spiritless labor can lead only to tragedy in the day of Christ is something the average Christian seems to have forgotten. But how about you?

Perhaps your doctrinal bias is away from belief in the crisis of the Spirit's filling. Very well, look at the fruit of such doctrine. What is your life producing? You are doing religious work, preaching, singing, writing, promoting, but what is the quality of your work? True; you received the Spirit at the moment of conversion, but is it also true that you are ready without a further anointing to resist temptation, obey the Scriptures, understand the truth, live victoriously, die in peace and meet Christ without embarrassment at His coming?

If, on the other hand, your soul cries out for God, for the living God, and your dry and empty heart despairs of living a normal Christian life without a further anointing, then I ask you: Is your desire all-absorbing? Is it the biggest thing in your life? Does it crowd out every common religious activity and fill you with an acute longing that can only be described as the pain of desire? If your heart cries "Yes" to these questions you may be on your way to a spiritual breakthrough that will transform your whole life.

It is in the preparation for receiving the Spirit's anointing that most Christians fail. Probably no one was ever filled without first having gone through a period of deep soul disturbance and inward turmoil. When we find ourselves entering this state the temptation is to panic and draw back. Satan exhorts us to take it easy lest we make shipwreck of the faith, and dishonor the Lord that bought us.

Of course, he cares nothing for us nor for our Lord. His purpose is to keep us weak and unarmed in a day of conflict. And millions of believers accept his hypocritical lies as gospel truth and go back to their caves like the prophets of Obadiah to feed on bread and water.

Before there can be fullness there must be emptiness. Before God can fill us with Himself, we must first be emptied of ourselves. It is this emptying that brings the painful disappointment and despair of self of which so many persons have complained just prior to their new and radiant experience.

I doubt whether anyone ever received that divine afflatus with which we are here concerned who did not first *experience a period of deep anxiety and inward agitation.*

Religious contentment is the enemy of the spiritual life always. The biographies of the saints teach that the way to spiritual greatness has always been through much suffering and inward pain. The phrase, "the way of the cross," though it has come in certain circles to de-note something very beautiful, even enjoyable, still means to the real Christian what it has always meant, the way of rejection and loss. No one ever enjoyed a cross, just as no one ever enjoyed a gallows.

The Christian who is seeking better things and who has to his con-sternation found himself in a state of complete self-despair need not be discouraged. Despair with self, where it is accompanied by faith, is a good friend, for it destroys one of the heart's most potent enemies and prepares the soul for the ministration of the Comforter. A sense of utter emptiness, of disappointment and darkness can (if we are alert and wise to what is going on) be the shadow in the valley of shadows that leads on to those fruitful fields that lie further in. If we misunder-stand it and resist this visitation of God, we may miss entirely every benefit a kind heavenly Father has in mind for us.

There must come a total of self-disvaluation, a death to all things without us and within us, or there can never be a real filling with the Holy Spirit.

> *The dearest idol I have known,*
> *Whate'er that idol be,*
> *Help me to tear it from Thy throne,*
> *And worship only Thee.*

We sing this glibly enough, but we cancel out our prayer by our refusal to surrender the very idol of which we sing. To give up our last idol is to plunge ourselves into a state of inward loneliness which no gospel meeting, no fellowship with other Christians, can ever cure. For this reason, most Christians play it safe and settle for a life of compromise. They have some of God, to be sure, but not all; and God has some of them, but not all. And so they live their tepid lives and try to disguise with bright smiles and snappy choruses the deep spiritual destitution within them.

One thing should be made crystal clear: The soul's journey through the dark night is not a meritorious one. The suffering and the loneliness do not make a man dear to God nor earn the horn of oil for which he yearns. We cannot buy anything from God. Everything comes out of His goodness on the grounds of Christ's redeeming blood and is a free gift, with no strings attached.

What the soul agony does is to break up the fallow ground, empty the vessel, detach the heart from earthly interests and focus the attention upon God. If we cooperate with God, He will take away the natural comforts which have served us as mother and nurse for so long and put us where we can receive no help except from the Comforter Himself. He will tear away that false thing the Chinese call "face" and show us how painfully small we really are. When he is finished with us, we will know what our Lord meant when He said, *"Blessed are the poor in spirit."* (Matthew 5:3

Be sure, however, that in these painful chastenings we shall not be deserted by our God. He will never leave us nor forsake us, nor will He be wroth with us nor rebuke us. He will not break His covenant nor alter that which has gone out of His mouth. He will keep us as the apple of His eye and watch over us as a mother watches over her child. His love will not fail even while He is taking us through this experience of self-crucifixion so real, so terrible, that we can express it only by crying, *"My God, my God, why hast thou forsaken me?"* (Psalm 22:1; Matthew 27:46; Mark 15:34)

Now let us keep our theology straight about all this. There is not in this painful stripping one remote thought of human merit. The "dark night of the soul" knows not one dim ray of the treacherous light of self-righteousness. We do not by suffering earn the anointing for which we yearn, nor does this devastation of soul make us dear to God nor give us additional favor in His eyes. The value of the stripping experience lies in its power to detach us from life's passing interests and to throw us back upon eternity. It serves to empty our earthly vessels and prepare us for the inpouring of the Holy Spirit.

The filling with the Spirit, then, requires that we give up our all, that we undergo an inward death, that we rid our hearts of that centuries-old accumulation of Adamic trash and open all rooms to the heavenly Guest.

The Holy Spirit is a living Person and should be treated as a person. We must never think of Him as a blind energy nor as an impersonal force. He hears and sees and feels as any person does. He speaks and hears us speak. We can please Him or grieve Him or silence Him as we can any other person. He will respond to our timid effort to know Him and will ever meet us over half the way.

However wonderful the crisis experience of being filled with the Spirit, we should remember that it is only a means toward something greater: that greater thing is the lifelong walk in the Spirit, indwelt, directed, taught and empowered by His mighty Person. And to continue thus to walk in the Spirit requires that we meet certain conditions. These are laid down for us in the sacred Scriptures and are there for all to see.

The Spirit-filled walk demands, for instance, that we live in the Word of God as a fish lives in the sea. By this I do not mean that we study the Bible merely, nor that we take a "course" in Bible doctrine. I mean that we should "meditate day and night" (Psalm 1:2) in the sacred Word, that we should love it and feast upon it and digest it every hour of the day and night. When the business of life compels our attention we may yet, by kind of blessed mental reflex, keep the Word of Truth ever before our minds.

Then, if we would please the indwelling Spirit, we must be all taken up with Christ. The Spirit's present work is to honor Him, and everything He does has this for its ultimate purpose. And we must make our thoughts a clean sanctuary for His holy habitation. He dwells in our thoughts, and soiled thoughts are as repugnant to Him as soiled linen to a king. Above all we must have a cheerful faith that will keep on believing however radical the fluctuation in our emotional states may be.

The Infilling

All that has gone before is by way of soul preparation for the divine act of infilling. The infilling itself is not a complicated thing. While I shy away from "how to" formulas in spiritual things, I believe the answer to the question "How can I be filled?" may be answered in four words, all of them active verbs. They are these: (1) surrender, (2) ask, (3) obey, (4) believe.

Surrender: "I beseech you therefore, brethren, by the mercies of God, that ye present your bodies a living sacrifice, holy, acceptable unto God, which is your reasonable service. And be not conformed to this world: but be ye transformed by the renewing of your mind, that ye may prove what is that good, and acceptable, and perfect, will of God" (Rom. 12:1,2).

Ask: "If ye then, being evil, know how to give good gifts unto your children: how much more shall your heavenly Father give the Holy Spirit to them that ask him?" (Luke 11:13).

Obey: "We are his witnesses of these things; and so is also the Holy Ghost, whom God hath given to them that obey him" (Acts 5:32).

Complete and ungrudging obedience to the will of God is absolutely indispensable to the reception of the Spirit's anointing. As we wait before God we should reverently search the Scriptures and listen for the voice of gentle stillness to learn what our Heavenly Father expects of us. Then, trusting to His enabling, we should obey to the best of our ability and understanding.

Believe: This only would I learn of you, Received ye the Spirit by the works of the law, or by the hearing of faith?" (Gal. 3:2).

While the infilling of the Spirit is received by faith and only by faith, let us beware of that imitation faith which is no more than a mental assent to truth. It has been a source of great disappointment to multitudes of seeking souls. True faith invariably brings a witness.

But what is that witness? It is nothing physical, vocal nor psychical. The Spirit never commits Himself to the flesh. The only witness He gives is a subjective one, known to the individual alone. The Spirit announces Himself to the deep-in spirit of the man. The flesh profiteth nothing, but the believing heart knows. Holy, holy, holy.

One last thing: Neither in the Old Testament nor in the New, nor in Christian testimony as found in the writings of the saints as far as my knowledge goes, was any believer ever filled with the Holy Spirit who did not know he had been filled. Neither was anyone filled who did not know when he was filled. And no one was ever filled gradually.

Behind these three trees many half-hearted souls have tried to hide like Adam from the presence of the Lord, but they are not good enough hiding places. The man who does not know when he was filled was never filled (though of course it is possible to forget the date). And the man who hopes to be filled gradually will never be filled at all.

In my sober judgment the relation of the Spirit to the believer is the most vital question the church faces today. The problems raised by Christian existentialism or neo-orthodoxy are nothing by comparison with this most critical one. Ecumenicity, eschatological theories— none of these things deserve consideration until every believer can give an affirmative answer to the question, "Have ye received the Holy Ghost since ye believed?"

And it might easily be that after we have been filled with the Spirit we will find to our delight that the very filling itself has solved the other problems for us.

The Spirit indwelt life is not a special deluxe edition of Christianity to be enjoyed by a certain rare and privileged few who happen to be made of finer and more sensitive stuff than the rest. Rather, it is the normal state for every redeemed man and woman the world over. It is *"the mystery which hath been hid from ages and from generations, but now is made manifest to his saints: to whom God would make known what is the riches of the glory of this mystery among the Gentiles; which is Christ in you, the hope of glory."* (Colossians 1:26-27)

Faber, in one of his sweet and reverent hymns, addressed this good word to the Holy Spirit:

> *Ocean, wide flowing Ocean, Thou*
>
> *Of uncreated Love;*
>
> *I tremble as within my soul*

I feel Thy waters move.

Thou art a sea without a shore;

Awful, immense Thou art;

A sea which can contract itself

Within my narrow heart.

Fellowship with the Spirit

Most people would like to have the power and the peace of the Spirit with a lot of other qualities, and gifts and benefits the Holy Spirit may bring. Now the question is: can we afford to walk with the Spirit? And, are we going to walk with Him? And the answer is: we cannot walk with Him until or unless we are in agreement with Him.

Taking it out of the realm of the Spiritual for just a little bit, and thinking about two people, which is what is meant here; "Can two people walk together except they be agreed?"

That takes us back to the old days when men made long journeys on foot. One man said, "I'm going to a certain town." The other one said, "I am too. When are you going?" "I'm going tomorrow."

Then the question, would they go together, or would each one go off by himself. Now if they were going to go walk together as the disciples at Emmaus, there were a few things they are going to have to agree upon.

One is their direction and the other is their destination, of course. "You're going to such a town?" "Yes." "Well I am not." Therefore, they would have to shake hands and depart because two men cannot walk together when one man is going to one city and the other to another. At least they cannot for very long.

Then they would have to agree on which path to take if there were several paths. They would have to agree on the rate of speed. One man said, "I am a very fast walker," and the other man said, "I just clump along; I hardly make it at all." They would say, "Well there's no use for us to walk together, because I am so slow I would bore you." The other man would say, "No, I'm so fast that I would trouble you." So, they would not go together.

Then, they would have to agree they wanted to walk together; did they want to walk together. There are some people that, if I was going to walk from here to Hamilton, I would just as soon walk by myself. I love them all right, and I pray for them, but I do not find them edifying companions. You have to decide whether you want to walk together or not, whether it is advantageous to both parties concerned, whether there is incompatibility that might render the trip unpleasant.

For two to walk together voluntarily, they must be one. They must agree on the things that matter if they are going to walk together. Now that bears upon the subject I want to talk about, and you will quickly see how it bears.

How to cultivate the Spirit's companionship—how to walk with the Holy Ghost.

Some people are just not ready to hear what I have to say, and of that I am convinced. Some are not willing to give up all to obtain all. They are not willing to turn toward God and walk with Him. They are facing both ways. John Bunyan talked about Mr. Facing Both Ways. A great many Christians, even gospel Christians, are facing two directions at once and they are not willing to go along one way. They want some of the world and some of Christ. They allow the Lord to disturb their way, but they also disturb the Lord's way. And they do not get together on this. And there is no use of us talking about being filled with the Spirit and walking in the Spirit unless we are willing to give up all to obtain all.

Then there are Christians, and a lot of them in our gospel churches, that want Christianity for its insurance value. That is, they want the care and protection that God gives them now. They want avoidance of hell at the time of death. They want the guarantee of heaven at last.

To get this, they are willing to support the church, and missions, and other religious projects financially. And, who would not be willing to pay his insurance, if he knew it would help him in the hospital if he got sick; or got into an accident, it would pay his widow a lot of money if he died. Who wouldn't be willing to pay and support that kind of insurance?

Christianity, to some people, is simply there for its insurance value. They want its protection and what it has to offer and guarantee of heaven at last. Now I say, they are willing to support it, and they are willing to abstain from certain gross or pleasures. I do not think you will have much difficulty getting the average person to quit gambling if he has been a gambler. I don't think you'll have much trouble getting the average man separated from a lot of the fleshly things, because you know there are a lot of sinners that don't do certain sins; there's a lot of sinners.

My father used tobacco, both smoking and chewing for, I guess, fifty years. One day he looked at the stuff and had a sudden revulsion of feeling. He said what a dirty mess that is after all, and he turned his back on it, and never touched it again, even until he died. He was not converted for many years after that. Between the time he gave it up and the time he was converted, a period of perhaps eight to ten years, he just did not like the stuff anymore.

Not every sinner is dirty, not every sinner is a rascal; not every sinner cheats on his wife; not every sinner refuses to pay his debts. There are honorable men and good men and honest men, who will tell the truth if it hurts, right out in the world, that have no hope of eternal life nor heaven to come, that are not followers of the Lord; they're just decent people. The idea that everybody is a wicked rascal and a scoundrel is all wrong. I have known some of the finest men who are not Christians.

 I know a man in Chicago who is so good that everybody wants to make a Christian out of him, but he steadfastly refuses, and says, I am not a Christian, I am not a Christian. But he is so good that he puts to shame many Christians. He does not claim that he is winning his way to heaven; it is not a question of the old morality that the evangelists talk about. He does not believe in that. He just knows he is lost, but he is also a man of incorruptible character; he is a good man. And of course, many Christians are willing to give up the grosser things and live in a reasonably decent way.

Some people are not ready for this message. Their conception of religion is social and not spiritual. They water down the strong wine of the New Testament until it has no tang in it anymore. They water it down with their easygoing opinion. They are very broad-minded, they imagine, but the fact is they are so broad-minded, they cannot walk on the narrow way.

And many Christians now are more influenced by Hollywood than they are Jerusalem. That is just as sure as you live, that is their spirit; their mood is more like Hollywood than it is Jerusalem. If you were to sit them down in Jerusalem, they would wander around, even as in the days of Christ, and would not feel at home. Take them out to that nest of iniquity in California, and they would say, I wonder who she is. I wonder if she is one of the stars. They would be quite at home there, because their mood, the texture of their mind, has been created for them by twentieth century entertainment and not by the things of God.

Some people would like to be filled with the Spirit for the thrill of it.

They want to be thrilled and they would pay almost any price to get the thrill. However, they will not die to themselves, to the world, or to the flesh. Hence, for these, what I have to say now will have no sympathetic meaning whatsoever. You just cannot have any meaning, because they have not come over into the region where God can get to them.

But I know there are some who have said, "Jesus, I my cross have taken all to leave and follow thee." And from somewhere has come a longing, a blessed aspiration; a deep longing, a yearning after God that is so real and so wonderful and so pain filled that they know what I am talking about sympathetically.

And I do not know who they are. It is impossible for me to know. Among the things God has not done for me is to give me the ability to put my finger on a man and say, thou art the man, or, thou art not the man. God keeps His mysteries and His secrets from me to some extent, so I cannot tell you who they are.

Thank God, there are always some.

You see, there is a difference between knowing doctrine intellectually and knowing it sympathetically. Anybody can learn the catechism and know the doctrine intellectually. And we have Bible Conferences all over the United States and all over Canada, all over England, all over Scotland and Wales and all over the world. Wherever Christianity is heard, we have Bible Conferences, and we take a week to ten days to study the Word. And its good and you can get a hold of the Word of God intellectually. It is quite another thing to let the Word of God reach you sympathetically; that is, your heart goes out sympathetically to the Word of God and it reaches you sympathetically.

I think there are some here like that and maybe more than I think, for I will break down and tell you something. I am not an optimist except in the long-range eschatological sense. If you do not know what eschatological means ask me. I do not know whether I do, but I am thinking now about the long-range future event. I am an optimist in that, but not too much of an optimist when it comes to things of now. I am likely to underrate than overrate. You will find that out now if I stay around here much longer. But maybe there are more people hungry for God than I know. Maybe so, and I sincerely hope so; and if there are and if there is even, one then I want to give this second half of my talk now.

If you are a hungry person and Christ is more to you than an insurance against hell, and Christianity is to you more than an opportunity to mingle socially with good people; If God is real to you and Christ is real, and your heart is longing after God and you want the best God has and your heart is open to the Holy Spirit's incoming, then I want to give you a few thoughts now.

First, the Holy Spirit is a living person. That is, He can be known in increasing degrees of intimacy. This is the second time I have said, this but I want to emphasize it tonight that since the Holy Spirit is a personality, He is never fully known in one encounter. One of the biggest mistakes we can possibly make is to imagine that, by coming to know God in the new birth and receiving the Spirit of adoption whereby we cry Abba Father, we know all we can know about God. And people of our persuasion make the second mistake, which is being filled with the Holy Ghost after conversion.

Some think they know all there is to know about the Holy Spirit. Oh, my friend, you have just started. For God's personality is so infinitely rich and manifold, that it will take a thousand years of close search and intimate communion even to begin to know the outer edges of the glorious nature of God. So that when we talk about communion with God and fellowship with the Holy Spirit, we are talking about that which begins now, but which grows and increases while life lasts. Everything else being equal, if you are a seeker after God. as I hope you are, and you go on in obedience, you will know God much better five years from now than you know Him now.

And if you do not know Him better now than you did five years ago, then you have pretty much wasted five years of your life. You know it is possible to do that. Jacob wasted twenty years of his life and then went back to the altar, had his second experience by the river Jaboc, had his name changed from Jacob to Israel and went on from there. However, twenty years was taken out of his life.

And I find Christian people that have wasted their lives. They have been converted to Christ, but they have not gone on to know the Lord increasingly. They have accepted the cold level of things round about them being normal. Well, there is untold loss and failure. People are a little more modest about that now.

I think Mussolini, the Roman Empire and a few other things rather blew up in our faces, and we are not quite as sure of ourselves as we used to be when it comes to prophecy. I used to hear young fellows, you know, who weren't dry behind their ears yet, get up and talk about reigning over five cities, how many crowns they were going to wear and all that sort of thing. They were not going to wear any crowns nor reign over any city, but they thought they were. They had it all worked out theologically.

But they were not getting on to know God. They were just opening the Word, as they call it, and teaching the Word about five crowns of the Christian and that sort of thing.

Well, they are suffering loss nevertheless; suffering loss because they are bogged down in their teachings and have not gone on to know God for Himself.

So the Holy Spirit is a living person. And as He is a living Person, you can know Him and fellowship with Him; whisper to Him and have His voice whisper back to you in some love text that you know, or some love hymn, and whisper back to you, so that walking with the Spirit can become a habit with you. Something you can do so that you can be in His presence, conscious of His presence, so you will not always have to talk.

I think I mentioned before that there are two kinds of friendship. There is the tentative and uncertain kind of friendship that does not allow you to sit down and look at a magazine when you come to their house, or just sit down and snooze. They have to be entertaining you, because they do not know you well enough and you do not know them well enough to relax. Nobody relaxes. You are company; they are entertaining you and somebody must be talking every minute in order for you to know you are welcome.

After you know these people, and you grow in the knowledge of each other and your friendship becomes bigger, sweeter, and broader, you can go to their house or they to yours and not say anything for ten minutes at a time and nobody will think you are mad. Then your friendship has passed by the place where it has to be kept up by chatter.

And I believe it is possible to get to a place where we can know God so intimately that we do not always have to be chattering to God. We can pray and inwardly we do pray, but we do not have to all the time.

I remember once riding with a preacher, and we had to make a certain engagement where I was to preach. We were riding along in the rain some years ago, and in those days the cars were not closed up much underneath, and when it splashed, it got water in the points, and the car would stop.

This poor fellow was driving, and I was sitting beside him, and it was raining hard. The car would sputter, and he would pray to beat the band: "Oh, God, keep it going, keep it going, God."

Then, when it would stop sputtering, he would talk a little; and then it would sputter some more, he would pray a little more, and he was just so worried there; he and God had not had any understanding about that at all. Apparently, they were not closely enough acquainted so they could relax, or at least he could relax. I think God was relaxed about the whole thing, but my preacher friend was not.

It is possible to know Him in increasing intimacy. I want to ask you, do you know God better now than you knew him a year ago? I want to ask you, do you know God more intimately, warmly, than you knew Him a year ago? Are you growing in grace?

I do not say has it been an even motion upward, like a flight of a plane, gaining altitude. Because it has been my experience and experience of Bible Christians, and I find the same thing true in Biography, that we do not take off from a ramp, mount straight up toward God and continue to mount. We zigzag up, and zigzag up.

But the point is, when the zigs and the zags have been ironed out, are you nearer to God now than you were a year ago? Are you closer to the heart of God now? Allowing for the bumps that you had during the time, allowing for the times of coldness, are you closer now than you were a year ago. If you are not, something is seriously wrong, and you should consider doing something about it no later than tonight.

Now, how can I cultivate that holy fellowship?

I will tell you; be engrossed with Christ. Honor Christ and the Holy Ghost will honor you. You remember that Jesus, on that last day of the feast, lifted up His voice and cried and said *"He that believeth on me, as the scripture hath said, out of his belly shall flow rivers of living water. (But this spake he of the Spirit, which they that believe on him should receive: for the Holy Ghost was not yet given; because that Jesus was not yet glorified.)"* (John 7:38-39 KJV) The pouring out of the Holy Ghost depended upon and waited upon, the glorification of Jesus Christ the Lord.

When Pentecost was fully come, Peter got up to preach a sermon and reflected back to that same passage and said, *"Be it known unto you all, and to all the people of Israel, that by the name of Jesus Christ of Nazareth, whom ye crucified, whom God raised from the dead, even by him doth this man stand here before you whole."* (Acts 4:10 KJV)

Always remember that you will know the Spirit more intimately as you make more of Jesus Christ the Lord. For Jesus said the Holy Spirit would take the things of His and show them unto us.

We walk with the Holy Ghost when we walk with Christ. For Christ will always be where He is honored. The Holy Ghost will always honor the one who honors the Savior Jesus Christ the Lord. Let us honor Him by giving Him His right title. Let us call Him Lord, let us believe He is Lord, let us call Him Christ. Let us believe He is Christ, and let us get away from this cheap Jesus dear kind of stuff that pulls Christianity down to the world of erotica and makes it half-sexy.

Let's get rid of that whole silly business and remember, "God has made this Jesus, whom ye crucified, Lord and Christ; and set Him at His own right hand and put all things under His feet and made Him to be head over all things of the church; and He shall reign from the river to the ends of the earth." This is the Christ we adore and let us be careful to honor Christ; always honor Christ. Honor Him by obedience, honor Him by witness, honor Him by testimony; and as we all honor Christ, then we will fellowship with the Holy Ghost.

Again, to know the Holy Spirit in increasing intimacy of companionship, we must walk in righteousness. Walk in righteousness, because we might as well face up to it my brethren; God cannot possibly have fellowship with a man or woman that is not living right or not walking right.

We have magnified grace all out of proportions to the Bible. Paul says, with weeping, that men had turned the grace of God into lasciviousness, and we have done the same thing now. We are so afraid that we will reflect upon the all sufficiency of grace that we dare tell Christians that we have to live right.

But remember, Paul in the Holy Ghost wrote his epistles and, in those epistles, he laid down holy inward ethics; moral rules for the inward Christian. Read it in Romans and Corinthians and Ephesians, and

Colossians and Galatians, and see whether it does not all add to the same thing. Read the Sermon on the Mount and the other teachings of Jesus, and see if He does not expect His people to be clean and right.

I wrote an editorial for the Alliance Witness, and at the same time, it was printed in London in a magazine, "The Life of Faith." I was rather amused when I discovered they were taking me to task. I was over here having a nice time; over there they were writing hot letters back and forth to each other about me.

One fellow said, "Tozer does not distinguish between discipleship and salvation; to be a disciple and to be a Christian." Another responded by saying, "He said you could be a Christian without being a disciple."

Whoever said you could be a Christian without being a disciple? You cannot be a Christian without being a disciple. The idea that I can come to the Lord by grace, and have all my sins forgiven, and have my name written in heaven, have the carpenter go to work on a mansion in my Father's house and at the same time I can raise hell on my way to heaven. I say it is impossible. It is unscriptural, it is not found in the Bible at all. You are not saved by your good works, no never are we saved by our good works, but we are not saved apart from good works. We are saved by faith in Jesus Christ alone, but out of that, springs immediately goodness and righteousness.

Flowers do not bring spring, but you cannot have spring without flowers. It is not the birds that bring the summer, but you have no summer without birds. It is not righteousness that saves me but salvation brings righteousness. The man who is not ready to live right, he is not saved; he will not be saved, and he will be deceived in that great day.

I spent some thirty-one years in a town that is, or was for a good many years, the Mecca of evangelical Christianity. It is pretty hard to preach this there without getting into trouble. But I preached it all right and kept on preaching it; and before I left, I was being heard by everybody. And the very persons who before had held another view were listening to me, and I am preaching it to you now, that we must walk in righteousness.

I cannot for the life of me see how it is possible that we can support the doctrine that Christians ought to be good people. Christians ought to be the best people in the world. And I could not believe a man is on his way to heaven when he's performing such deeds as indicate that, logically he ought to be on his way to hell.

So walk in righteousness and see to it that you do. And make your thoughts a clean sanctuary; to God our thoughts are part of us. The Spirit is all seeing and all hearing and all loving and pure, and He cannot endure thoughts of malice. Can you imagine a man with malicious thoughts in his heart having companionship with the loving Holy Ghost? No, it is impossible that he should. Can you imagine a man bloated with egotism knowing the Holy Spirit with anything like intimacy? No, he could not possibly do it.

Can you imagine a man who is a deceiver ever having any fellowship with the Spirit? Never. Can you imagine it? It is folly to believe it my friend. If you have habitually given over to thinking dirty thoughts, you are habitually without the communion of the Holy Ghost, let me tell you that. Keep your mind pure.

This gossip business; God deliver us from it. But it is here, we have to deal with it and if we do not deal with it, it will deal with us. I have even found that prayer groups are gossipers. Some sister will get up and say in a high, shocked voice, "Now I would not mention this except I want you to pray." The old hypocrite, that is not it at all. She is just gossiping and she wants to do it publicly.

And she says now, "I want you to pray for Mrs. Jones. I looked in the window as I went by and Mr. Jones and Mrs. Jones were arguing, and I'm sure there's a fight in that home." And the old sister would love to have had a bug in there, a microphone, and just heard the whole thing. She would not smoke a cigarette, and she sneers down her holy nose at any woman who would smoke, but she loves a bit of dirty gossip.

Then she says, "I was filled with the Holy Ghost at such and such a Camp Meeting." Well, she's never gone on from there. In fact, she has gone back from there, because one of the things the Spirit of God will do for a person is to make them so they don't want to gossip about people. They may be driven; it may be necessary for them to talk about things that are not good and they may have to sometimes if they're on committees, or they're choosing a teacher or anything else. They may be compelled. I have been many a time compelled to deal frankly with people's characters, but that is one thing. It is quite another thing to love to hear gossip about people.

Make your thoughts a clean sanctuary. Clean out the sanctuary the way old Hezekiah did back there. They had dirtied up that sanctuary, and when Hezekiah took over, he got all his priests together and it took them several days and they carried out all the filth and burned it. Threw it over the bank and got rid of it and went back and sanctified the temple, and then the blessed God came and they had their worship again. Well then, I would also suggest that you seek to know Him in His Word.

Now remember that He inspired the Word and He will be revealed in the Word. I have no place in my sympathies for Christians who neglect the Word, ignore the Word or get any revelations apart from the Word. This is the book, after all, my friends, "Oh Word of God incarnate, Oh wisdom from on high, Oh Word unchanged, unchanging, Oh light of our dark sky." This is the book; and if we know the book, well enough we will have an answer to every problem in the world that touches us.

But some people get far off the track. I stay by the Word; I want to preach the Word and love the Word and make the Word everything. Read it much, read it often, brood over it, think over it, meditate over it, meditate on the Word of God day and night.

When you wake at night, think of a verse. When you get up in the morning, no matter how you feel, think of a verse and make the Word of God everything. Because the Holy Ghost wrote the Word, and if you will make a lot of the Word, He will make a lot of you. He will make a lot of the Word and He will make a lot of Himself to you.

For it is through the Word that God reveals Himself. This is not a dead book between covers; this is a living book. God wrote it and it is still alive. This book is still alive; it is a living, vibrant book. God is in this book. The Holy Ghost is in this book.

And if you want to find Him go into the book. If you want to find the Shepherd, you know where to look, find His sheep and you will find the Shepherd. And if you want to find the Holy Ghost, go where the Holy Ghost inspires in the book itself and you will find Him there. I know it is possible to know doctrine without the Spirit, and I have said that a while ago. It is possible to know the doctrine intellectually, not know it sympathetically, and still not find the Holy Ghost there.

But do not try to cultivate the Spirit without the Word. There is an awful lot of that now. A lot of humanism over-larded with a lot of paganism, over-larded again with a bit of esoteric religion, nature, poetry and philosophy of sweet old ladies and all that. Now that will not do friends, it is not enough, it is not enough. I believe in great hymns but all these cute little things that people write when they should have been looking after the baby, and then they get them into print and want me to place them in my Bible and read them. I will not do it. I would rather pass them over, forget them, go to the Word itself.

Then I would say, cultivate the art of recognizing the presence of the Spirit, every place, all the time. The Spirit of the Lord fills the world. The blessed Holy Spirit is here and you cannot walk out away from where He is. You cannot hide away from Him; David tried it in 139th Psalm. He said, "I found that I could not do it. I went up into heaven and you were there, if I go down to hell, you are there and if I go to the uttermost parts of the sea, you are there, and if I say darkness hides me I find God shines even in the darkness." He said, "I could not get away from God." If you are interested in Him, you will find Him where you are. The presence all about you.

I would recommend that you find out what it is that has been hindering you. Nobody wants to be asked that question. But find out what it is that has been hindering your life. You have not progressed; you do not know God as well as you did or at least any better than you did. What is the trouble? Well, the Lord's people do many borderline things. Let me give you an example.

A friend of mine who is now in heaven, H.W. were his initials. He used to write me a letter and say, "Dear A.W." and sign it, "H.W." A dead soul, a dear man of God.

He came in one time from a missionary convention where he had been the preacher and he told me this.

"Brother Tozer, we are in desperate need of revival out in a certain section in the Alliance."

And I said, "Is that so. What lead you to that conclusion?"

"Well," he said, "here is an example. We were having our missionary convention throughout the week, and it went along all right until Friday night. Friday night the pastor came to me and said, 'Now tonight, we are going to shorten the meeting a little bit. You'll be on last, and I want you to quit so that we can be out of the building with the lights out by ten minutes of nine.'

"He told me, 'The missionary will talk, and we cannot always tell how long the missionary will go, and there will be singing and some announcements and an offering and then you will preach. I do not care how long you preach, only one thing, remember tonight, we must be out of the building at ten minutes of nine.'

"I said all right, and I got through about a quarter of nine and they sang a verse and prayed and went home. The building was empty ten minutes of nine. Later on, I found out why this pastor was shortening the meeting and rushing us out of the church. Friday night was the night the fights came on television and the pastor could not give up his Friday night fights."

Two bruisers knocking each other's brains out up there, if they ever had any to start with, and he had to see that. It had so hooked him, it had so hooked him that he closed a missionary convention even though Jesus said to "tarry until ye be endued with power from on high, and then go and preach the gospel to every creature." And these missionaries were there, giving up everything to go, but this pastor had to shorten the meeting to see the fights.

In a hotel room in New York City, I set one time with nothing in the wild world to do and I watched a fight. I am not saying it is a deeply sinful thing to do, but in the context, it was deeply sinful and iniquitous for a pastor to be so caught up in a thing that he grieved the Holy Ghost and quenched the Spirit and insulted God.

Now brethren, find out what it is; it may not be that with you. And the rule is, does this hide the face of Jesus a little bit from me? Does this chill my heart a little? Does this take the joy out of my Spirit? Does this make the Word of God a little less sweet? Does this make earth a little more desirable?

If you answer yes to those questions, then you're going to have to do some repenting, and some cleaning up before the blessed Holy Ghost will come to your heart and warm it and refresh it and make it fragrant with His presence. This is how we cultivate the Spirits friendship.

Somebody said, "That kind of living, Mr. Tozer, is narrow and old fashioned, and I would be deprived of so many things." Now, is not that just terrible that you would be deprived of a few cheap trinkets if you followed God.

What would you think of a woman who would balk at going down the aisle to marry the man she is supposed to love if she said to him, "Listen, at home I've got a big house, my father looks after me; I don't have to work and I just can't give up these comforts to marry anybody." That is exactly what we are telling the Lord. We are saying, "Lord, these are things that I have always enjoyed doing and I am not going to make any changes for Thy sake."

You will never hear any talk back from God, never. As the Welsh preacher said, "God is a gentleman and He always knocks at the door; He has never pushes it open and He never barges in. He waits to be wanted, He waits to be invited and He waits to be loved." And if you would rather have the cheap trinkets of the world than to walk with the King of Glory, you can have it dear friend. You will get no argument from me; you will get none from God.

Remember, He is a Person and can be cultivated just as you cultivate a friend. Remember, you must be engrossed with the Person of Christ for He glorifies Christ. Remember, you must walk in righteousness, for God will not fellowship anyone who deliberately lives in sin. Make your thoughts a clean sanctuary; be clean inside as well as out. Seek to know Him in the Word. Live in the Word so the Holy Ghost can live in you. And cultivate the art of recognizing the presence of the Lord and of the Holy Spirit everywhere, at all times.

Then find out what is hindering you and put it out of your life. Well, that is simple enough, is it not? There is nothing fanatical about it. Only I wonder if we are going to pay the price.

Marks of the Holy Spirit's Working

The Christian Scriptures, particularly the gospel of John, contain two truths that appear to stand opposed to each other. One is that whosoever will may come to Christ. The other is that before anyone can come there must have been a previous work done in his heart by the sovereign operation of God.

The notion that just anybody, at any time, regardless of conditions, can start from religious scratch, without the Spirit's help, and believe savingly on Christ by a sudden decision of the will, is wholly contrary to the teachings of the Bible. God's invitation to men is broad but not unqualified. The word "whosoever" throws the door open wide, indeed, but the church in recent years has carried the gospel invitation far beyond its proper bounds and turned it into something more human and less divine than that found in the sacred Scriptures.

What we tend to overlook is that the word "whosoever" never stands by itself. Always its meaning is modified by the word "believe" or "will" or "come." According to the teachings of Christ no man will or can come and believe unless there has been done within him a prevenient work of God enabling him so to do.

In the sixth chapter of John our Lord makes some statements that gospel Christians seem afraid to talk about. The average one of us manages to live with them by the simple trick of ignoring them. They are such as these:

(1) Only they come to Christ who have been given to Him by the Father (John 6:37).

(2) No one can come of himself; he must first be drawn by the Father (John 6:44).

(3) The ability to come to Christ is a gift of the Father (John 6:65).

(4) Everyone given to the Son by the Father will come to Him (John 6:37).

It is not surprising that upon hearing these words many of our Lord's disciples went back and walked no more with Him. Such teaching cannot but be deeply disturbing to the natural mind. It takes from sinful men much of the power of self-determination upon which they had prided themselves so inordinately. It cuts the ground out from under their self-help and throws them back upon the sovereign good pleasure of God, and that is precisely where they do not want to be. They are willing to be saved by grace, but to preserve their self-esteem they must hold that the desire to be saved originated with them; this desire is their contribution to the whole thing, their offering of the fruit of the ground, and it keeps salvation in their hands where in truth it is not and can never be.

Admitting the difficulties this creates for us, and acknowledging that it runs contrary to the assumptions of popular Christianity, it is yet impossible to deny that there are certain persons who, though still unconverted, are nevertheless different from the crowd, marked out of God, stricken with an interior wound and susceptible to the call of Christ to a degree others are not.

About the teaching as a mere doctrine I am not much concerned, but I am keenly interested in learning how to identify such persons. No man is ever the same after God has laid His hand upon him. He will have certain marks, and though they are not easy to detect perhaps we may cautiously name a few.

One mark is a *deep reverence for divine things*. A sense of the sacred must be present or there can be no receptivity to God and truth. This mysterious feeling of awe precedes repentance and faith and is nothing else but a gift from heaven. Millions go through life unaffected by the presence of God in His world. Good they may be and honest, but they are nevertheless men of earth, "finished and finite clods," and proof against every call of the Spirit.

Another mark is a *great moral sensitivity*. Most persons are apathetic, insensitive to matters of the heart and the conscience, and so are not salvable, at least not in their present condition. But when God begins to work in a man to bring him to salvation He makes him acutely sensitive to evil. Inward repulsion toward the swine pen that rouses the prodigal and starts him back home is a gift of God to His chosen.

Another mark of the Spirit's working is a *mighty moral discontent*. In spite of our effort to make sinners think they are unhappy the fact is that wherever social and health conditions permit the masses of mankind enjoy themselves very much. Sin has its pleasures (Heb.

11:25) and the vast majority of human beings have a whale of a time living. The conscience is a bit of a pest but most persons manage to strike a truce with it quite early in life and are not troubled much by it thereafter.

It takes a work of God in a man to sour him on the world and to turn him against himself; yet until this has happened to him he is psychologically unable to repent and believe. Any degree of contentment with the world's moral standards or his own lack of holiness successfully blocks off the flow of faith into the man's heart. Esau's fatal flaw was moral complacency; Jacob's only virtue was his bitter discontent.

Again before a man can be saved he must feel a *consuming spiritual hunger*. Anyone who lives close to the hearts of men knows that there is little spiritual hunger among them. Religion, pious talk, yes; but not real hunger. Where a hungry heart is found we may be sure that God was there first. *"Ye have not chosen me, but I have chosen you"* (John 15:16).

The Church and the Spirit

"Concerning spiritual gifts, brethren," wrote Paul to the Corinthians, "I would not have you ignorant."

Certainly Paul meant nothing derogatory by this. Rather, he was expressing a charitable concern that his fellow believers should be neither uninformed nor in error about a truth so vastly important as this one.

For some time, it has been evident that we evangelicals have been failing to avail ourselves of the deeper riches of grace that lie in the purposes of God for us. As a consequence, we have been suffering greatly, even tragically. One blessed treasure we have missed is the right to possess the gifts of the Spirit as set forth in such fullness and clarity in the New Testament.

Before proceeding further, however, I want to make it plain that I have had no change of mind about the matter. What I write here has been my faith for many years. No recent spiritual experience has altered my beliefs in any way. I merely bring together truths which I have held during my entire public ministry and have preached with a fair degree of consistency where and when I felt my hearers could receive them.

In their attitude toward the gifts of the Spirit Christians over the last few years have tended to divide themselves into three groups.

First, there are those who magnify the gifts of the Spirit until they can see little else.

Second, there are those who deny that the gifts of the Spirit are intended for the Church in this period of her history.

Third, there are those who appear to be thoroughly bored with the whole thing and do not care to discuss it.

More recently we have become aware of another group, so few in number as scarcely to call for classification. It consists of those who want to know the truth about the Spirit's gifts and to experience whatever God has for them within the context of sound New Testament faith. It is for these that this is written.

Every spiritual problem is at bottom theological. Its solution will depend upon the teaching of the Holy Scriptures plus a correct understanding of that teaching. That correct understanding constitutes a spiritual philosophy, that is, a viewpoint, a high vantage ground from which the whole landscape may be seen at once, each detail appearing in its proper relation to everything else. Once such vantage ground is gained, we are in a position to evaluate any teaching or interpretation that is offered us in the name of truth.

A proper understanding of the gifts of the Spirit in the Church must depend upon a right concept of the nature of the Church. The gift problem cannot be isolated from the larger question and settled by itself.

The true Church is a spiritual phenomenon appearing in human society and intermingling with it to some degree but differing from it sharply in certain vital characteristics. It is composed of regenerated persons who differ from other human beings in that they have a superior kind of life imparted to them at the time of their inward renewal.

They are children of God in a sense not true of any other created beings. Their origin is divine and their citizenship is in heaven. They worship God in the Spirit, rejoice in Jesus Christ and have no confidence in the flesh. They constitute a chosen generation, a royal priesthood, a holy nation, a peculiar people.

They have espoused the cause of a rejected and crucified Man Who claimed to be God and Who has pledged His sacred honor that He will prepare a place for them in His Father s house and return again to conduct them there with rejoicing. In the meantime, they carry His cross, suffer whatever indignities men may heap upon them for His sake, act as His ambassadors and do good to all men in His name.

They steadfastly believe that they will share His triumph, and for this reason they are perfectly willing to share His rejection by a society that does not understand them. And they have no hard feelings—only charity and compassion and a strong desire that all men may come to repentance and be reconciled to God. This is a fair summary of one aspect of New Testament teaching about the Church. But another truth more revealing and significant to those seeking information about the gifts of the Spirit is that the Church is a spiritual body, an organic entity united by the life that dwells within it.

The Body of Christ

Each member is joined to the whole by a relationship of life. As a man's soul may be said to be the life of his body, so the indwelling Spirit is the life of the Church.

The idea that the Church is the body of Christ is not an erroneous one, resulting from the pressing too far of a mere figure of speech. The apostle Paul in three of his epistles sets forth this truth in such sobriety of tone and fullness of detail as to preclude the notion that he is employing a casual figure of speech not intended to be taken too literally.

The clear, emphatic teaching of the great apostle is that Christ is the Head of the Church which is His body. The parallel is drawn carefully and continued through long passages. Conclusions are drawn from the doctrine and certain moral conduct is made to depend upon it.

As a normal man consists of a body with various obedient members with a head to direct them, so the true Church is a body, individual Christians being the members and Christ the Head.

The mind works through the members of the body, using them to fulfill its intelligent purposes. Paul speaks of the foot, the hand, the ear, the eye as being members of the body, each with its proper but limited function; but it is the Spirit that worketh in them (1 Cor. 12:1-31).

The teaching that the Church is the body of Christ in 1 Corinthians 12 follows a listing of certain spiritual gifts and reveals the necessity for those gifts.

The intelligent head can work only as it has at its command organs designed for various tasks. It is the mind that sees, but it must have an eye to see through. It is the mind that hears, but it cannot hear without an ear.

And so with all the varied members which are the instruments by means of which the mind moves into the external world to carry out its plans.

As all man's work is done by his mind, so the work of the Church is done by the Spirit, and by Him alone. But to work He must set in the body certain members with abilities specifically created to act as media through which the Spirit can flow toward ordained ends. That in brief is the philosophy of the gifts of the Spirit.

It is usually said that there are nine gifts of the Spirit. (I suppose because Paul lists nine in 1 Corinthians 12.) Actually Paul mentions no less than 17 (1 Cor. 12:4-11, 27-31; Rom. 12:3-8; Eph. 4:7-11). And these are not natural talents merely, but gifts imparted by the Holy Spirit to fit the believer for his place in the body of Christ. They are like pipes on a great organ, permitting the musician wide scope and range to produce music of the finest quality. But they are, I repeat, more than talents. They are spiritual gifts.

Natural talents enable a man to work within the field of nature; but through the body of Christ God is doing an eternal work above and beyond the realm of fallen nature. This requires supernatural working.

Religious work can be done by natural men without the gifts of the Spirit, and it can be done well and skillfully. But work designed for eternity can only be done by the eternal Spirit. No work has eternity in it unless it is done by the Spirit through gifts that He has Himself implanted in the souls of redeemed men.

For a generation, certain evangelical teachers have told us that the gifts of the Spirit ceased at the death of the apostles or at the completion of the New Testament. This, of course, is a doctrine without a syllable of biblical authority back of it. Its advocates must accept full responsibility for thus manipulating the Word of God.

The result of this erroneous teaching is that spiritually gifted persons are ominously few among us. When we so desperately need leaders with the gift of discernment, for instance, we do not have them and are compelled to fall back upon the techniques of the world.

This frightening hour calls aloud for men with the gift of prophetic insight. Instead, we have men who conduct surveys, polls and panel discussions.

We need men with the gift of knowledge. In their place we have men with scholarship—nothing more.

Thus we may be preparing ourselves for the tragic hour when God may set us aside as so-called evangelicals and raise up another movement to keep New Testament Christianity alive in the earth. Say not, "We be children of Abraham. God is able of these stones to raise up children unto Abraham."

The truth of the matter is that the Scriptures plainly imply the imperative of possessing the gifts of the Spirit. Paul urges that we both "covet" and "desire" spiritual gifts (1 Cor. 12:31, 1 Cor. 14:1). It does not appear to be an optional matter with us but rather a scriptural mandate to those who have been filled with the Spirit.

But I must also add a word of caution.

The various spiritual gifts are not equally valuable, as Paul so carefully explained.

Certain brethren have magnified one gift out of seventeen out of all proportion. Among these brethren there have been and are many godly souls, but the general moral results of this teaching have nevertheless not been good.

In practice it has resulted in much shameless exhibitionism, a tendency to depend upon experiences instead of upon Christ and often a lack of ability to distinguish the works of the flesh from the operations of the Spirit.

Those who deny that the gifts are for us today and those who insist upon making a hobby of one gift are both wrong, and we are all suffering the consequence of their error.

Today there is no reason for our remaining longer in doubt. We have every right to expect our Lord to grant to His Church the spiritual gifts which He has never in fact taken away from us, but which we are failing to receive only because of our error or unbelief.

It is more than possible that God is even now imparting the gifts of the Spirit to whomsoever He can and in whatever measure He can as His conditions are met even imperfectly. Otherwise the torch of truth would flicker out and die.

Clearly, however, we have yet to see what God would do for His Church if we would all throw ourselves down before Him with an open Bible and cry, "Behold Thy servant, Lord! Be it unto me even as Thou wilt."

A grave manmade error is the belief that there is nothing to be disturbed about because Christ carries the supreme authority of God. Therefore, everything is taken care of and we don't need to be bothered.

Christ does carry the supreme authority of God; but to ignore that authority is a grave offense.

Some will say, "God will take the initiative; I do not need to do anything. I believe that God will always be the aggressor." By the way, I believe that, too; but remember, God has already taken the initiative when He sent His holy Son, Jesus Christ, into the world, and when He sent the Holy Spirit down to take the things of Christ and show them unto us. So God has already taken the initiative. If God cannot disturb us, He cannot move us. If He cannot move us, He cannot save us. If He cannot get us concerned about the things of God, He cannot do anything at all for us.

The Omniscient God

His understanding is infinite.

PSALM 147:5

Neither is there any creature that is not manifest in his sight: but all things are naked and opened unto the eyes of him with whom we have to do.

HEBREWS 4:13

These texts say that God's understanding is limitless, that His knowledge is perfect, and that there isn't a creature anywhere in the universe that isn't plainly visible to His sight. Nothing is shut before the eyes of God. That is what is called divine omniscience, one of the attributes of God. An attribute, as I have said before, is something which God has declared to be true about Himself.

God has declared by divine revelation that He is omniscient, that He knows everything. The human mind staggers under this truth when we consider how much there is to know and how little we know. Ralph Waldo Emerson said, for example, that if a man were to start reading the books in the British Library on the day he was born and read day and night for seventy years, without taking time to eat or sleep, he would only be able to read a small section of the books in that collection.

Even those who know so very much, know so very little. Dr. Samuel Johnson, the great English lexicographer, was known as the most learned man in England. When he was compiling the first English dictionary, he defined a hock (the middle joint on a horse's rear leg) as a horse's knee (the middle joint on a horse's front leg). Some time afterward, at a party somewhere, a society lady turned to the great doctor and thought she would get a rise out of him.

She said, "Dr. Johnson, why did you define a hock as a horse's knee?"

He said, "Ignorance Madam, sheer ignorance."

He was the most learned man in all England, but he admitted that he was ignorant on some things. Will Rogers said, "Everybody is ignorant—only on different subjects." And when it comes to knowing anything, I get very discouraged when I go to a library. I come out feeling as if I know absolutely nothing at all—which, if the truth were known, is a lot nearer to the facts than I would like to admit!

When I received one of the honorary degrees that have been bestowed on me, I said, "The only thing that is learned about me is this pair of glasses." If a man has his hair slicked back and a pair of learned-looking glasses, they call him a doctor. We don't know very much, really, and when we consider the great God who knows all there is to know with perfection of knowledge, we stagger under that. The weight of the truth is too much for our minds.

When Sir Isaac Newton, the great English scientist, was an old man, someone said to him, "Dr. Newton, you must have a tremendous store of knowledge."

He responded, "I remind myself of a little boy walking along the seashore picking up shells. The boy has a handful of shells in his little hand, but all around him is the vast seashore stretching all directions as far as the eye can see. All that I know is simply a handful of seashells, but the vast universe of God is filled with knowledge that I do not possess."

When we talk about God's knowledge of everything, we're talking about a rational approach to God. There are two ways to approach God: theologically and experientially. You can know God experientially and not know much theology, but it's good to know both. The more you know about God theologically the better you can know Him experientially.

A rational approach to God is what I can get into my head. You can't get too much into your head, really. And what I can get into my head about God isn't very much at all. But that's one way to approach God—through theology, through your intellect, through doctrine. But the purpose of doctrine is to lead you to see and to know God experientially, to know God for Himself, for yourself. But until we know God theologically, we're not likely to know God very well experientially.

Reason can best think of God in negatives. In other words, as the old mystic devotional writers used to say, we can best conceive of God by conceiving of what He is not. We can always know what God is not, but we can never know quite what God is. The greatness of God's mind leaves all our soaring thoughts behind. God is ineffable (incapable of being expressed in words), inconceivable and unimaginable.

What's *unimaginable* mean? It just means that you can't think of what God is like. One man I heard about used to kneel down in front of a chair and say, "Jesus, You take the chair." And then he'd imagine Jesus on the chair. I've never cared for that sort of thing. I've never cared much for religious pictures, either. I'm always horrified when I see Michelangelo's picture of the creation. God Almighty is portrayed as an old, bald-headed man lying on a cloud, pointing His fiery finger down at Adam, as Adam comes to life. Can you imagine conceiving of God as a bald-headed old man? I think the artist would have done us a wonderful favor if he had reverently laid down his brushes and never tried to paint the figure of God.

We don't know what God is like. If you can think it, it isn't God. If you can think it, it is an idol of your own imagination. If you don't believe what I'm saying, read what the Holy Ghost said in First Corinthians 2:7-11:

But we speak the wisdom of God in a mystery, even the hidden wisdom, which God ordained before the world unto our glory: which none of the princes of this world knew. … But as it is written, Eye hath not seen, nor ear heard, neither have entered into the heart of man, the things which God hath prepared for them that love him. But God hath revealed them unto us by his Spirit: for the Spirit searcheth all things, yea, the deep things of God. For what man knoweth the things of a man, save the spirit of man which is in him? even so the things of God knoweth no man, but the Spirit of God.

And you'll never know what I'm talking about without the illumination of the Holy Ghost. When we crowded the Holy Ghost out of the Church and took in other things instead, we put out our own eyes. The Church is filled with blind men who cannot see because the Holy Ghost has never opened their eyes.

Lydia could not believe in Christ till the Lord had opened her eyes. Those disciples could not believe on Christ there on the Emmaus Road until He had opened their eyes. No one can see God nor believe in God until the Holy Ghost has opened their eyes. When we grieve and quench the Holy Ghost, when we neglect Him, crowd Him out and substitute other things for Him, we make blind men out of ourselves.

We must come to God reverently, on our knees. You always see God when you're on your knees. You never see God when you're standing boldly on your feet, in full confidence that you'll amount to something. God is unimaginable, inconceivable; you cannot get into your head what God is like, or visualize God's being. The rule is, if you can think it, God isn't like that.

God is not like anything you know, except the soul of a man. It was old Meister Eckhart, the German saint, who said that the soul of a man was more like God than anything in the universe. He made man in His own image; you can't see a man's soul and therefore you've never seen anything that is like God. You've never heard or touched anything that is like God, except within your own heart. God lies beyond our thoughts, towers above them, escapes them and confounds them in awful incomprehensible terror and majesty.

As I said, we are driven to the use of negative statements when speaking about God. When we speak of the self-existence of God, we say God has no origin. When we speak of God's eternity, we say God has no beginning. When we speak of the immutability of God, we say God has no change. When we speak of the infinity of God, we say that God has no limits. When we speak of the omniscience of God, we say that God has no teachers and cannot learn. All these are negative statements.

We would cut down the length of a lot of prayers if we recognized that God can't learn anything. The average church deacon may take up to twenty minutes every Sunday giving God lessons. But God can't learn because He already knows everything there is to know. He knows the thing that you're trying to tell Him and He knows it more perfectly than you do.

Well now, the Scripture takes this negative method too. Scripture says the Lord "fainteth not, neither is weary" (Isaiah 40:28) and that He "cannot lie" (Titus 1:2). It says, "I am the LORD, I change not" (Malachi 3:6). It says, "with God nothing shall be impossible" (Luke 1:37). And it says God "cannot deny himself" (2 Timothy 2:13). And all of those things are, of course, negative. Now in case somebody charges me with being negative in my outlook, let me read what our Lord Jesus Christ said here in the 11th chapter of Matthew:

At that time Jesus answered and said, I thank thee, O Father, Lord of heaven and earth, because thou hast hid these things from the wise and prudent, and hast revealed them unto babes. Even so, Father: for so it seemed good in thy sight. All things are delivered unto me of my Father: and no man knoweth the Son, but the Father; neither knoweth any man the Father, save the Son, and he to whomsoever the Son will reveal him. (Matt 11:25-27)

I cannot know with my head but I can have it revealed to my spirit, by the Holy Spirit. My knowledge of God is not the knowledge Paul referred to when he said,

And I, brethren, when I came to you, came not with excellency of speech or of wisdom, declaring unto you the testimony of God. For I determined not to know any thing among you, save Jesus Christ, and him crucified. And I was with you in weakness, and in fear, and in much trembling. And my speech and my preaching was not with enticing words of man's wisdom, but in demonstration of the Spirit and of power: that your faith should not stand in the wisdom of men, but in the power of God. (1 Corinthians 2:1-5)

Remember, this was a Grecian city; they thought in the context of Greek philosophy. Paul was a thinker too, a philosopher. But he said, "When I came to you, I came not using big words; I came determined to know nothing except Jesus and Him crucified."

You see, if your faith stands in human argument, someone who is a better arguer can argue you out of it again. But when the Spirit of God reveals truth to your heart and God manifests that truth to your heart, nobody can argue you out of it. If you know God through Jesus Christ the Lord, nobody can argue you out of it.

I have learned that nobody knows enough to contradict the Word of God successfully. Some people think they do, but they don't. One man told me, "Sometimes I am troubled by the foundations of my faith. But when I'm worried about the foundations, I dive deep down into the Bible and examine the foundations. And I always come back out and shake the water out of my hair and sing, 'How firm a foundation, ye saints of the Lord, is laid for your faith in His excellent Word!'" You may be sure nobody knows enough to contradict the Word of God.

Divine omniscience, among other things, means that God knows Himself. According to Paul, "the things of God knoweth no man, but the Spirit of God" (1 Corinthians 2:11). God thus knows Himself. And since God is the source and author of all things and contains all things, it follows that God knows all things. In one effortless act, God knows instantly and perfectly all things that can be known.

It's good sometimes to be around people who can do things easily. They don't have to strain until the muscles stand out in their necks. For example, I like to hear someone take a high note and hold it. We have a record of a great Italian soprano; there seems to be no top to her voice at all! She goes way up over the staff, up over the top of the book, up to the ceiling and then threatens to soar away into the blue. And she never seems to strain one muscle at all.

It's nice to know somebody can do something without effort. Most of us have an awful time getting anything done. I've written some books and it's cost me sweat and blood. But when it comes to God, He does everything effortlessly. God never strains. He never says, "Oh, this is going to be a hard one!" Never! God is able to do it as easily as He is able to do anything else.

In the same way, God, in one effortless act, knows instantly (not a little at a time, but instantly and perfectly) all things that can be known. That's why I say that God cannot learn. As I said before, if we realized that God couldn't learn, we could shorten our prayers quite a bit and step up their power. There is no reason to tell God things that He knew before you were born!

God knows the end from the beginning and He knew it long before it happened. Long before your parents met, God knew what you would be doing at this very moment. Before your grandparents met, before England was a nation, or the Roman Empire dissolved, or the Roman Empire was formed, God knew all about us. He knew everything about us—every hair on our head, our weight, our name, our past. And He knew it before we were born.

He knew it before Adam was. And when Adam walked in the garden with God, God knew all about Adam, all about Eve, all about their sons, all about the human race. God never gets astonished, astounded or surprised, because He already knows. You can walk down the street, turn the corner and get the surprise of your life. But God never turned the corner and got surprised, for the simple reason that God was already around that corner before He turned it. God already knew before He found out! God knows all things.

It's nice to sit down and talk things over with God. The Psalms are full of that, as well as the history of the saints. It's good to talk to God, even though we are talking to God about things He already knows. But this idea of giving God a lecture, I never did believe very much in it.

I love to hear people pray, but I don't like to hear them pray the same prayers, day in day out. That's why I don't always go to all the prayer meetings I might. I know what they're going to say anyhow, so why not just say as the cowboy did when he wrote his prayer on a card and stuck it on the head of his bed. When he got into bed, he said, "Lord, them's my sentiments," and went to sleep! I don't know why I should have to go and spend a half hour on my bony knees listening to some old deacon lecture God for three quarters of an hour. God already knows! He cannot learn.

If there was anything God could learn, it would mean that God didn't know it before. If He didn't know it before, then He didn't know everything. And if He didn't know everything, He wouldn't be perfect, and if He isn't perfect then He isn't God.

The God who can learn anything is not God. God already knows all that can be learned, all there is to know, and He knows it instantly and perfectly and without strain or self-consciousness. He knows it all. That's what Paul meant in Romans 11:33-36:

O the depth of the riches both of the wisdom and knowledge of God! how unsearchable are his judgments, and his ways past finding out! For who hath known the mind of the Lord? or who hath been his counseller? Or who hath first given to him, and it shall be recompensed unto him again? For of him, and through him, and to him, are all things: to whom be glory for ever. Amen.

It says God has no counselor—another negative expression. God had no teacher. He never went to school. Who could teach God? Could God call in an archangel and say to him, "Archangel, I'd like to get a little information about this"? We know the President of the United States has people all out over the country with their ears to the ground, providing him information. Politicians are always trying to find out what the public is saying. And as soon as a politician finds out what the public is saying, he gets up and boldly announces, "Them's my convictions." And he gets elected. But he got elected by finding out what the public wanted him to know.

Can you imagine God calling in a seraphim and saying, "There's a galaxy out there so many billion light years away that kind of got out of my range; I'd like to have you visit it and bring back information so I'll know how to run my universe"? I couldn't worship a God like that; I'd pity Him. I'd say, "What a wonderful big universe, but such a small god!" No, God never sends anybody out after information. God has it instantly, perfectly and effortlessly. God knows all that there is. He never discovers anything and He never finds out anything. He never wanders around seeking information.

One challenge to this that may come to mind is that passage back in Genesis, "*I will go down now and see if these things be true, about that city of Sodom.*" (see Gen 18:21) Do you know why God said that? God—who had made Sodom, who knew the end from the beginning—knew what was true, but He was dealing with people.

Sometimes our Lord asked people questions, but He didn't ask for information, "*because he knew all men… he knew what was in man.*" (John 2:24-25) He just asked to draw the man out, the same as if you said to a five-year-old boy, "Johnny, who was the first President of the United States?" You're not asking him in order to gain information! Reminds me of the boy who started his first day of school. He came home and announced that he wasn't going back.

"Why?" asked his mother.

"Well," he said, "the teacher is the dumbest woman I've ever seen in my life. She knows absolutely nothing at all. She has to ask me everything!"

So God said, "I'll go down now and I'll see" and He asked a question. Jesus our Lord asked questions of His disciples, but He already knew the answers. So God knows!

It is a great consolation to me that God knows instantly, effortlessly and perfectly all matter and all matters, all law and all laws, all space and all spaces, all principles and every principle, all minds, all spirits and all souls. God knows all causes and all relations, all effects and all desires, all mysteries and all enigmas, all things unknown and hidden. There are no mysteries to God.

There are many things that are mysteries to you and me. "*And without controversy great is the mystery of godliness: God was manifest in the flesh.*" (1 Timothy 3:16) Theologians throughout the centuries have reverently tried to discover how the infinite, inimitable God could condense Himself into the form of a man. It's a great mystery. We don't know, but God knows and God isn't worried about it. That's why I can live a good and peaceful Christian life, even though I am not a man that takes things very easy.

I'm not worried about these satellites they're shooting around the earth. I'm not worried about Kruschev (former leader of the Soviet Union) or any of the rest of those fellows over there with names you can't pronounce. Because God's running His world and He knows all about it. He knows where these men will die, He knows where they will be buried and He knows when they'll be buried. God knows all hidden things, "dwelling in the light which no man can approach unto" (6:16).

And He also knows His people. You who have fled for refuge to Him, Jesus Christ the Lord, He knows you, and you're never an orphan. A Christian is never lost, though he may think he is. He may be in the north woods hunting deer and lose his way, but he's not lost; the Lord knows where he is. The Lord knows all about him. The Lord knows about his health and knows about his business. Isn't it a consolation to you that our Father knows it all?

> *He knows, He knows*
>
> *The storms that would my way oppose*
>
> *He knows, He knows*
>
> *And tempers every wind that blows.*

Is that a consolation to you? It is to me. It's a consolation to me to know that

> *I know not where His islands lift*
>
> *Their fronded palms in air;*
>
> *I only know I cannot drift*
>
> *Beyond His love and care.*

Is your blood pressure running high? Are you worried? Maybe you don't know what to do and you think nobody else knows. Well, I have news for you. He that is perfect in knowledge is with you and He knows! If you'll trust Him He'll bring you out all right. He is perfect in knowledge and will lead you through. And when you come out you will know that everything God did was right.

"He hath done all things well." (Mark 7:37) Do you believe it? Do you believe that God's dealing with you is right? Maybe the person you married didn't turn out to be the angel that you thought. Well, God knows all about you. And He knows that even if it was a mistake, it is a mistake that God can overrule. God can take nothing and make something out of it. God can take your mistakes and polish those mistakes.

Have you heard the old story about the beautiful cathedral window that was vandalized? Some children threw pebbles at it and it was cracked all over. They sent for one of the finest artists in the land and asked, "What can you do?"

He said, "Leave it to me." And he went to work with his fine chisels and began cutting the glass. He made artistic lines wherever there was a break, turning each crack into a beautiful thing. When it was all over, the sun shone in on one of the most beautiful pieces of art glass in the world.

I remember that passage back in the book of Psalms that says, *"Though ye have lien among the pots, yet shall ye be as the wings of a dove covered with silver, and her feathers with yellow gold."* (Psalms 68:13) Now what does that mean? It shows the picture of a poor dove that fell down among the old cans and broken pots, the place where old junk is thrown out. Perhaps someone shot an arrow, hit this little dove and she went tumbling down and landed there. She wasn't dead, but she was in bad shape. So she got some sunshine and pecked a few seeds here and there, waiting for nature to heal her wing. And one day the sun was bright and the other birds were up in the air, so she tried out her engines, revved up her motor and off she went.

As she circled around, someone said, "Oh, look at the beautiful dove, shining in the silver!"

"Yes," another said, "look at the gold along the edges of her wing."

She had just been down in the junk pile a little while before, but now she arose by the grace of God into the sunshine. That was David's way of saying that God can take nothing, can take the poor wrecks of you and me, and can change us and make us into doves with wings of silver and gold.

God even knows the unblessed man, the man without God. If I were speaking to an unsaved man, the first thing that I would say to him is, God knows you by name. Isaiah 45:4 says, "I have even called thee by thy name… though thou hast not known me." God knows your name and He knows you fully. According to Psalm 139, He knows why you're rejecting His Son. He knows your secret sins.

You know, a person with a secret sin can get away with it for a long time. I read in the newspaper about men who for twenty years have been robbing banks. You can rob banks or juggle your books, but one person knows about it, and that's God. God knows your excuses and your real reasons, those that you hardly know yourself. He knows your checkered past and your future.

He knows the last place that you're going to lie down. He knows the name of the driver of the hearse that's going to drive you out to that last place. He knows all about it. He knows and sees what you don't know or see. He knows why you're not a Christian, why you're not following His Son. So why not put yourself in His keeping now?

There's a great old Latin hymn in which the writer reminds Jesus Christ (I'll put this in my own words), "Lord Jesus, remember why You came this way. I'm the reason." That's your plea, no matter how bad you are, no matter how crooked, deceptive and deceitful, no matter how you've assimilated and dissimilated. You can always go to Jesus Christ and the Lord will take you and receive you to Himself. What wonderful news— *"This man receiveth sinners, and eateth with them."* (Luke 15:2)

We can't tell God anything He doesn't already know and we can't excuse ourselves for anything. Our reasons are paper-thin and God sees through them. But in spite of it, God loves you, God invites you and God will receive you. There is no reason why you shouldn't come.

Prayer After Ordination

Written in 1950, this chapter has been reprinted many times and widely circulated.

This is the prayer of a man called to be a witness to the nations. This is what he said to his Lord on the day of his ordination. After the elders and ministers had prayed and laid their hands on him he withdrew to meet his Savior in the secret place and in the silence, farther in than his well-meaning brethren could take him.

And he said: O Lord, I have heard Thy voice and was afraid. Thou hast called me to an awesome task in a grave and perilous hour. Thou art about to shake all nations and the earth and also heaven, that the things that cannot be shaken may remain.

O Lord, my Lord, Thou hast stooped to honor me to be Thy servant. No man taketh this honor upon himself save he that is called of God as was Aaron. Thou hast ordained me Thy messenger to them that are stubborn of heart and hard of hearing. They have rejected Thee, the Master, and it is not to be expected that they will receive me, the servant.

My God, I shall not waste time deploring my weakness nor my unfittedness for the work. The responsibility is not mine, but Thine. Thou has said, "I knew thee—I ordained thee—I sanctified thee," and Thou hast also said, "Thou shalt go to all that I shall send thee, and whatsoever I command thee thou shalt speak." Who am I to argue with Thee or to call into question Thy sovereign choice? The decision is not mine but Thine. So be it, Lord. Thy will, not mine, be done.

Well do I know, Thou God of the prophets and the apostles, that as long as I honor Thee Thou wilt honor me. Help me therefore to take this solemn vow to honor Thee in all my future life and labors, whether by gain or by loss, by life or by death, and then to keep that vow unbroken while I live.

It is time, O God, for Thee to work, for the enemy has entered into Thy pastures and the sheep are torn and scattered. And false shepherds abound who deny the danger and laugh at the perils which surround Thy flock. The sheep are deceived by these hirelings and follow them with touching loyalty while the wolf closes in to kill and destroy. I beseech Thee, give me sharp eyes to detect the presence of the enemy; give me understanding to see and courage to report what I see faithfully. Make my voice so like Thine own that even the sick sheep will recognize it and follow Thee.

Lord Jesus, I come to Thee for spiritual preparation. Lay Thy hand upon me. Anoint me with the oil of the New Testament prophet. Forbid that I should become a religious scribe and thus lose my prophetic calling. Save me from the curse that lies dark across the face of the modern clergy, the curse of compromise, of imitation, of professionalism. Save me from the error of judging a church by its size, its popularity, or the amount of its yearly offering. Help me to remember that I am a prophet—not a promoter, not a religious manager, but a prophet. Let me never become a slave to crowds. Heal my soul of carnal ambitions and deliver me from the itch for publicity. Save me from bondage to things. Let me not waste my days puttering around the house. Lay Thy terror upon me, O God, and drive me to the place of prayer where I may wrestle with principalities and powers and the rulers of the darkness of this world. Deliver me from overeating and late sleeping. Teach me self-discipline that I may be a good soldier of Jesus Christ.

I accept hard work and small rewards in this life. I ask for no easy place. I shall try to be blind to the little ways that could make life easier. If others seek the smoother path, I shall try to take the hard way without judging them too harshly. I shall expect opposition and try to take it quietly when it comes. Or if, as sometimes it falleth out to Thy servants, I should have grateful gifts pressed upon me by Thy kindly people, stand by me then and save me from the blight that often follows. Teach me to use whatever I receive in such manner that will not injure my soul nor diminish my spiritual power. And if in Thy permissive providence honor should come to me from Thy church, let me not forget in that hour that I am unworthy of the least of Thy mercies, and that if men knew me as intimately as I know myself they would withhold their honors or bestow them upon others more worthy to receive them.

And now, O Lord of heaven and earth, I consecrate my remaining days to Thee; let them be many or few, as Thou wilt. Let me stand before the great or minister to the poor and lowly; that choice is not mine, and I would not influence it if I could. I am Thy servant to do Thy will, and that will is sweeter to me than position or riches or fame and I choose it above all things on earth or in heaven.

Though I am chosen of Thee and honored by a high and holy calling, let me never forget that I am but a man of dust and ashes, a man with all the natural faults and passions that plague the race of men. I pray Thee, therefore, my Lord and Redeemer, save me from myself and from all the injuries I may do myself while trying to be a blessing to others. Fill me with Thy power by the Holy Spirit, and I will go in Thy strength and tell of Thy righteousness, even Thine only. I will spread abroad the message of redeeming love while my normal powers endure.

Then, dear Lord, when I am old and weary and too tired to go on, have a place ready for me above, and make me to be numbered with Thy saints in glory everlasting. Amen. AMEN.